# The Beauty and Glory of the Christian Worldview

# The Beauty and Glory of the Christian Worldview

Edited by
Joel R. Beeke

**Reformation Heritage Books**
Grand Rapids, Michigan

Published by
**Reformation Heritage Books**
2965 Leonard St. NE
Grand Rapids, MI 49525
616-977-0889 / Fax 616-285-3246
e-mail: orders@heritagebooks.org
website: www.heritagebooks.org

*Printed in the United States of America*
17 18 19 20 21 22/10 9 8 7 6 5 4 3 2 1

ISBN: 978-1-60178-552-7 (hardback)
ISBN: 978-1-60178-553-4 (e-pub)

*For additional Reformed literature, request a free book list
from Reformation Heritage Books at the above address.*

With heartfelt appreciation for

**Chris Hanna**

a great and faithful friend, and dear brother in Christ,
an excellent organizer for PRTS's annual conferences,
a diligent marketer and development director for the seminary,
with whom it is a joy to colabor for Christ's kingdom on earth.

# Contents

# Contents

# Preface

As we grow older, our vision tends to cloud. In some cases, cataracts develop. After the cataracts are removed, people often testify how they can see more clearly and with brighter colors. They gain a whole new view of the world. In a similar manner, when God saves a sinner, it's like he gains a new pair of eyes. Everything is clearer, brighter, and more beautiful. The sinner has gained a new worldview shaped by the Word of God. Over time, the Holy Spirit uses the Word to increasingly conform our worldview to the mind of Christ.

What is a worldview? To put it most simply, our worldview is like a pair of lenses through which we see and evaluate everything. It is the assumptions that control how we think, feel, and act. As Christian missionary and anthropologist Paul Hiebert (1932–2007) said, a worldview is "the fundamental cognitive, affective, and evaluative presuppositions a group of people make about the nature of things, and which they use to order their lives."[1] It is not just a pair of glasses or contact lenses that we can take off at will; a worldview is more like our eyes, an organic part of who we are. As Christ said, "The light of the body is the eye" (Matt. 6:22).

Just as we view a mountain differently when we stand at its base, climb to its summit, or fly over it in a helicopter, so the Christian may view life from different perspectives, for there are many facets to our lives. At the Puritan Reformed Conference held in August 2016, we

---

1. Paul G. Hiebert, *Transforming Worldviews: An Anthropological Understanding of How People Change* (Grand Rapids: Baker Academic, 2008), 15.

explored the Christian worldview from various angles. This book contains the substance of messages delivered at the conference.[2]

The first part lays down foundation stones upon which a Christian builds his understanding of the world around him. A Christian view of reality must begin with God. Derek Thomas starts at the beginning with the essential Christian doctrine of the Trinity. Michael Barrett's chapter follows with a beautiful and awe-inspiring perspective on God's supremacy gleaned from the book of Ecclesiastes. Then the chapter which I co-authored with Paul Smalley draws upon the writings of the Puritans to discover how faith in God's fatherly providence shapes our view of godliness, family, and church, with special attention given to Puritan views of economics and politics.

The second part of this book considers how basic biblical perspectives form the Christian's practical life. Derek Thomas discusses Colossians 3:1–17 to show how the Christian's battle against sin and pursuit of holiness arise from knowing who he is and who he will be in Jesus Christ. Mark Kelderman tackles the controversial subject of human sexuality to show how the Bible remains God's authoritative and sufficient Word in this age of confusion and wickedness. Brian Cosby teaches us how to view our suffering through the biblical lenses of God's sovereignty and loving purposes for His dear children.

In the third part of the book, Christian truth is ignited like fuel to energize the heart and motivate action. Charles Barrett's exposition of 1 Peter 1:1–9 motivates the believer to stride forward as a joyful pilgrim on his way to his heavenly homeland. Gerald Bilkes's message from Matthew 28 calls us to cast off fearful unbelief and to follow the risen Lord Jesus in our mission to live as disciples and make disciples of all nations. The book closes with Charles Barrett's stirring exhortation from Hebrews 12:1–3 to look unto Jesus—the heart of our worldview—and to run the race of the Christian life with eyes fixed on Him.

I would like to express my gratitude to the people who made the publication of this book possible: Chris Hanna for organizing and

---

2. Audio recordings may be accessed at SermonAudio.com (search under Puritan Conference 2016). David Murray's address is not included in this volume as it was committed to another book and publisher prior to his delivering it.

administrating the Puritan Reformed conference, Misty Bourne for assisting me in editing the chapters, Linda den Hollander for typesetting, Gary den Hollander for proofreading, and Amy Zevenbergen for the attractive cover design. Thanks, too, to Lois Haley for transcribing two of the addresses.

This book is just a sampling of the edifying messages presented each year at the Puritan Reformed Conference. We invite you to join us each August in Grand Rapids.[3]

May the Lord use these chapters to illuminate the eyes of your heart with a beautiful and glorious view of our God and His ways.

—Joel R. Beeke

---

3. More information about these conferences may be found at www.prts.edu.

# FOUNDATIONAL TRUTHS FOR THE CHRISTIAN'S MIND

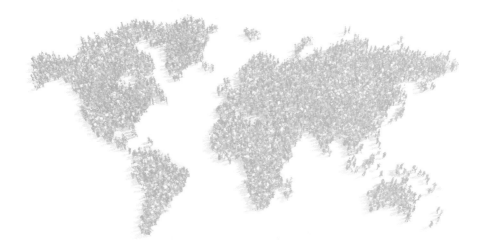

# CHAPTER 1

# The Christian Worldview
# of the Trinity

*Derek W. H. Thomas*

Apart from a disputed statement in John's first letter, there is no single text in the Bible that provides a clear statement of the doctrine of the Trinity, especially in its more familiar creedal form of a three-person, one-essence God. The notorious *Comma Johanneum*, the "Johannine comma" in 1 John 5:7 which is found in the King James Version, does enunciate a very clear witness: "For there are three that bear record in heaven, the Father, the Word, and the Holy Ghost: and these three are one." This text does not appear in many versions of the Bible. Part of the history of this text includes the publication of Erasmus's Greek New Testament in March 1516. Criticisms were made for the absence of this text. Erasmus famously responded that he had found no manuscripts that included it, adding that if one were to be found he would include it in subsequent editions. At length, a copy was found allegedly written to order in Oxford about 1520 by a Franciscan friar named Froy (or Roy), who took the disputed words from the Latin Vulgate. The text was subsequently included in the 1522 edition of Erasmus's Greek New Testament.[1] This is not the place to discuss this issue in detail, but differing traditions will weigh the legality of the Johannine text differently.

The doctrine of the Trinity is one of those doctrines (like the baptism of covenant children) that requires a more systematic approach

---

1. See Bruce Manning Metzger, *The Text of the New Testament: Its Transmission, Corruption, and Restoration* (Oxford: Oxford University Press, 1968), 101–103, 136. Six Greek manuscripts (according to the United Bible Society Greek New Testament) include this text. The earliest of these Greek witnesses, all of which depend on an earlier Latin tradition, can be dated to the twelfth century. See Stephen Smalley, *1, 2, 3 John, Word Biblical Commentary* (Waco, Tex: Word Biblical Commentary, 1984), 51:273.

than purely textual. We must ask the big-picture questions as to what the totality of Scripture teaches about God, and especially who it is that is referred to as God, to provide a total witness to God's nature and identity. What emerges in such a process is the clear statement that there is only one God, but there is more than one who is that one God. The Father is God; the Son is God; the Holy Spirit is God, and these three relate to each as separate and distinct subjects.

As we read from the Old Testament into the New Testament, we are confronted by certain data. First, and fundamentally, we are confronted by the insistence that there is only *one* God. One of the most fundamental passages in the Old Testament is the *Shema* of Israel, Deuteronomy 6:4: "Hear, O Israel: the LORD our God is one LORD." There is an allusion to it in 1 Timothy 2:5: "For there is one God." That is a Christian worldview in itself; there is *one* God, and one *only*. The *Shema*, for example, is the Bible's insistent testimony in opposition to the pluralistic cultures of the Ancient Near East. In a pluralistic society, and the wake of a late-modern hermeneutic of ambivalence, the Bible's insistence on the unity of God still comes as counter-cultural.

There is only one God, but there is *more than one who is that one God*. The data alone is explicit. Thus, the great commission in Matthew 28:19, 20: "Go ye therefore, and teach all nations, baptizing them in the name of the Father, and of the Son, and of the Holy Ghost: teaching them to observe all things whatsoever I have commanded you: and, lo, I am with you alway, even unto the end of the world. Amen." Or the benediction in 2 Corinthians 13:14: "The grace of the Lord Jesus Christ, and the love of God, and the communion of the Holy Ghost, be with you all. Amen." There is plurality in God in the sense that there is more to God than oneness. There is one *and* there is plurality within this one God. And that plurality is more than just a plurality of attributes or characteristics or aspects. There is a communion, there is a fellowship, a conversation within the being of the one God. There is distinction—personal distinction. One talks to and loves the other. And these distinctions are three and not just two. There is the Father. There is the Son. There is the Holy Spirit. And they exist simultaneously. They are not transformations from one to another.

Two questions arise as we make our way through the Christian worldview and the Trinity:

- What is the relationship of the Three to the One?
- What is the relationship of the Three to each other?

It is important to see that these two questions are raised not by philosophy but by the data of Scripture itself. Though the Bible does not answer these questions in creedal form, the Bible's own witness to the being of God demands that some answer be given to these questions. The doctrine of the Trinity is not the result of a "foreign" (e.g, Aristotelian, or Ramist) philosophy imposed as a grid upon Scripture. The need for a *doctrine* of the Trinity is something that is raised by Scripture itself. Scripture says there is one God; Scripture says there is more than one who is that one God. But how can both statements be true?

If Jesus is God, how does He as God relate to the Father and/or the Holy Spirit without positing more than one God, a statement of polytheism? One possible answer is that He is a *different* God. Both Judaism and Islam allege that Christianity is in essence polytheistic. Another answer is that Jesus is less than God. He is some sort of Superman, godlike but not quite God. His essence *begins*, as various forms of Arianism suggest.

These are some of the issues which led to the formulation of the Nicene Creed (and the later Niceno-Constantinopolitan Creed of AD 325 (or AD 381) insisted that that was not the case, that Jesus is "one Lord Jesus Christ, the Son of God, begotten of the Father [the only-begotten; that is, of the essence of the Father, God of God], Light of Light, very God of very God, begotten, not made, being of one substance with the Father."[2]

What evidence is there for a doctrine of the Trinity in the Scriptures, including the Old Testament? And, as a subset of this question, the following also receives particular attention: Is the doctrine of the Trinity found in the Old Testament? We recall Augustine's famous dictum: "The New Testament is latent in the Old (the 'bud'); the Old becomes patent in the New (the 'blossom')."[3]

---

2. The Niceno-Constantinopolitan Creed of AD 381 added a statement about the procession of the Holy Spirit: "The Lord, and Giver of Life, who proceeds from the Father, who with the Father and the Son together is worshipped and glorified, who spoke by the Prophets."

3. "Novum Testamentum in Vetere latet, Vetus in Novo patet." St. Augustine, *Quaestiones in Heptateuchum* 2, 73.

Many have pointed to the fact that in Genesis 1 you have the divine name *Elohim*, or "Lord" as it is frequently translated in English, using the lower case to distinguish it from the divine name given in Exodus 3, *Yahweh* (formerly and incorrectly rendered *Jehovah*, and translated in many English Bibles employing the upper case and small caps "LORD"). The point being that *Elohim* contains the distinctive Hebrew plural form (*-im*). God's name in the opening page of Scripture is a plural form. The statement in Genesis 1:26, "Let *us* make man in our image" (emphasis added), therefore takes on added significance. This has led many to conjecture a Trinitarian meaning in the divine name. Whilst this is intriguing, and most certainly convenient, the thought never occurred to any faithful and pious Jew in the Old Testament. They seemed to have read the plural in another way: as a denotation of majesty and splendor.[4]

Another example is found in the passage of Scripture where Isaiah "saw also the LORD sitting upon a throne, high and lifted up, and his train [glory] filled the temple. Above it stood the seraphims…. And one cried…Holy, holy, holy, is the LORD of hosts: the whole earth is full of his glory…. Then said I, Woe is me! for I am undone; because I am a man of unclean lips, and I dwell in the midst of a people of unclean lips: for mine eyes have seen the King, the LORD of hosts" (Isa. 6:1–3, 5). Some have (misguidedly) pointed to the threefold use of *trisagion* ("Holy, holy, holy") and more pertinently to the fact that the "Lord" whom Isaiah saw is specifically identified by John as Jesus Christ.[5] But it is the question that follows the vision that is somewhat telling: "Whom shall I send, and who will go for *us*?" (v. 8, emphasis added). Who is the "us" referred to here? There is plurality. And once again, pious Judaism did not concur. They saw majesty rather than plurality.

Then again we have the phenomenon, particularly in the time of the patriarchs, of the so-called "angel of the Lord," the *malak Yahweh* who appears and often in the text speaks from the point of view of the divine person suggesting that these are perhaps early

---

4. Note should be taken of Calvin's careful response to adumbrations of plurality in the term *Elohim* in his commentary on Genesis. *Commentaries on the First Book of Moses called Genesis*, 22 volumes, trans. Rev. John King (Edinburgh: Calvin Translation Society, 1847), 1:71–72.

5. John 12:41; cf. Isa. 6:1.

Christophanies, or revelations of Christ in physical form. Some have alluded to the personal *"hypostasis"* of Proverbs 8, where wisdom takes a "personal" form and is the basis for John's use of the term "Word" or *logos* in the prologue to his Gospel.

Others have pointed to Psalm 110:1, "The LORD said unto my Lord," made much of in the New Testament.[6] There is the "LORD" and then there is the "Lord," and they are engaged in conversation and dialogue with each other, commanding and responding. Does not this point to plurality with the Godhead?

The collective evidence leads some to suggest that in the Old Testament there is perceived to be an underlying suggestion "that all things owe their existence and persistence to a threefold cause."[7]

However, a stubborn fact remains. Despite this impressive evidence—*evidence* that is clearer this side of Pentecost for sure— there is not a single Old Testament author prepared to elaborate on the concept of plurality within the Godhead. The Old Testament remains stubbornly insistent on the unity of God rather than an idea of plurality within unity. The fundamental tenet of Old Testament Scripture remains the *Shema*—the declaration of God's oneness. One simply does not find any advocacy of plurality within unity in any of the great authors—neither Moses nor David nor Isaiah nor Ezekiel nor Jeremiah. The one constant in the Old Testament is the insistence that God is one—the unity of God—in opposition to the unambiguous polytheistic claims of the Ancient Near East.

### New Testament Evidence of the Deity of Jesus Christ
Turning to the New Testament revelation of God is therefore startling and surprising. For just as the Old Testament is insistently set on emphasizing the unity of God, the New Testament proclaims a God who is more than one, and does so without any clear example of debate or pushback. The Father is God. The Son is God. The Holy Spirit is God. These are statements readily discerned in the writings of the New Testament authors, all of them Jews, all of them committed to the ongoing validity of the Old Testament *Shema*. As

---

6. Matt. 22:43–44; Acts 2:33–36; Heb. 1:13 and alluded to in Matt. 22:63–64; Acts 5:30–31; 7:55–56; Rom. 8:34; 1 Cor. 15:54–55.

7. See B. B. Warfield's analysis of this claim in *Biblical Doctrines* (Edinburgh: Banner of Truth, 1988), 140ff.

B. B. Warfield insisted in the late nineteenth century, the doctrine of the Trinity appears in the New Testament not as something in the making but as something that has already been made.[8] There is no argument about Trinity in the New Testament. It is altogether assumed. There is no discussion about Trinity in the New Testament as there is about justification by faith. Paul must take up the doctrine of justification *apart from the works of the law* in Galatians and in Romans and argue it at length. There exists misinformation and opposition to this doctrine and the New Testament engages it. There is a prolonged argument in the New Testament about total depravity (eg. Rom. 2:1–3:20). But there is no argument or lengthy discussion of the doctrine of the Trinity in the New Testament. It is as though it is already assumed. There is no debate about it. This alone is one of the most puzzling features of the New Testament. And the reason is clear: so convinced were they of the deity of incarnate Jesus Christ that they do not question the validity of the statements "the Father is God" and "the Son is God." But neither do they assert that there are two Gods. Without precise formulation, the deity of Jesus forces into expression two truths: there is one God and there is more than one who is this one God.

Of course, there is none of the technical language that belongs to the third, fourth, and fifth centuries—(Latin) words like *trinitas, persona, essentia*, or *substantia*. These are technical words in the Western Church as it debated along with the Eastern Church's Greek words. Yet, despite the lack of this precision, the idea of the Trinity is manifestly evident in the New Testament.

As Paul, for example, expounds the work of redemption in Ephesians 1, how does he understand the accomplishment and the application of what Christ has achieved? Putting it another way, how does Paul fundamentally understand the way the gospel works in Ephesians 1? The answer is clear enough. Paul understands the accomplishment and application of redemption in Trinitarian terms. He writes about the predestination of the Father. He writes about the accomplishment of redemption by the incarnate Son. He talks about the application of redemption to the believer by the work of the Holy Spirit. And this he does in magnificent, lengthy discourse in Ephesians 1, without a comma or a period. Paul breaks all the

---

8. B. B. Warfield, *Biblical Doctrines*, 145f.

rules of grammar in the opening chapter of Ephesians in the interests of expounding a Trinitarian gospel. Indeed, such is the nature of what Paul writes that it is as though he were saying, "There is only one gospel and it is Trinitarian. To the degree that it is not Trinitarian is the degree to which it is another gospel. Unitarianism, or a Jesus-only gospel, does not work."

As we have said before, the doctrine (or worldview) of the Trinity in the New Testament emerges, essentially and primarily, because of the fundamental testimony to the deity of the Lord Jesus Christ. Jesus is more than just a Superman. He is more than just an adopted Son. He is the Lord of lords and King of kings. He is the only God there is. He is Yahweh.

Take, for example, the divine title *Theos*, God. John calls him *Theos* in the opening prologue of his Gospel: "In the beginning was the Word, and the Word was with God, and the Word was God" (John 1:1). John is writing basic and simple Greek. You can study Greek for twenty minutes, and if you have never read Greek in your life before, you can read John 1:1. And yet within these basic words and simple structure are some of the most profound thoughts that have ever been written. This Jesus is actually God! This Word who was made flesh (see John 1:14) and walked, talked, and breathed, who had a human mind, will, and affections, who ate, slept, and cried, and who could be killed and was pronounced dead is none other than God, none other than *Theos*! He is the only God there is.

Perhaps more fundamental and more profound is the attribution to the Lord Jesus of the title *Kurios*, which is the Greek translation of the Old Testament Hebrew word *Yahweh*, the divine, special, covenant name of God given in Exodus 3 and elaborated in Exodus 6. Thus, Paul's letter to the Philippians contains what looks like an early hymn/creed, *Carmen Christi*, the Song of Christ (Phil. 2:5–11). "Let this mind be in you, which was also in Christ Jesus: who, being in the form of God, thought it not robbery to be equal with God... he humbled [emptied] himself" (Phil. 2:5, 6, 8). And then, at the end of the song, we read these words: that one day, every knee will bow and tongue confess that Jesus Christ is "Lord" (Phil. 2:11). The Greek word for "Lord" is *kurios*, the word used in the Greek translation of the Hebrew Old Testament (the Septuagint, or LXX) to translate the divine name *Yahweh*. Jesus is Yahweh. That Jews like Paul could say this without thinking it blasphemy is one of the strongest arguments for the deity of Jesus. Christian-Jews like Paul were shaken to the core by the identity of Jesus and confessed him *kurios*. Jesus is God.

One surely would expect an explosion of misunderstanding and even opposition from a Jewish mindset that anyone would refer to Jesus as *Kurios*, as Lord, as Yahweh. But there is none from within the Christian community. Now New Testament critical scholarship has been saying for 150 years that the attribution of *Kurios* to Jesus is a Gentile phenomenon, not a Jewish phenomenon, that it has been imposed upon the Bible, rewritten by later additions to the text. That is the amazing thing about the New Testament. There is no discussion, no debate, no opposition within the Christian community of the New Testament as to the identity of Jesus as Lord, as Yahweh. You can go further and talk about the "I Am" sayings in John's Gospel, reflecting as they do the fundamental statement in Exodus 3:14 where the Lord reveals Himself as an exposition of Yahweh, meaning "I AM THAT I AM." Jesus is saying, "I *Am*; I am *He*."

Then there's the attribution of the title *Son of God* to consider, that extraordinary moment at Caesarea Philippi in Matthew 16:13, perhaps one of the key verses of the entire New Testament, and as important a text as Genesis 3:15. We read in Matthew 16:13: "Whom do men say that I the Son of man am?" Some answered "Elijah," "Jeremiah," "John the Baptist risen from the dead." But Peter says, "Thou art the Christ, the Son of the living God" (v. 16). And Jesus replies, "Flesh and blood hath not revealed it unto thee, but my Father which is in heaven" (v. 17). He does not deny the attribution that He is the Son of God. There is also that moment at the baptism of Jesus, that moment of the transfiguration of Jesus where the audible word of the Father comes and says, "This is my beloved Son" (Matt. 3:17).

There is also the use of the term *Son of man*. And here we must not make the fundamental assumption that "Son of God" means His deity and "Son of man" means His humanity. Such a distinction is simplistic and wrong. "The Son of man" is a description that comes from Daniel 7 and is an attribution of deity. This is a description of God; it is a *divine* title.

**The Deity of the Holy Spirit**

There are two indispensable facts to keep in mind: that early Christians believed that Jesus was divine, and that Jesus believed Himself to be divine. There is no trace of a merely human Jesus in the New Testament. In addition, there are the descriptions in the New Testament about the deity of the Holy Spirit. Is the Holy Spirit a person, capable of fellowship and communication, contemporaneous with and in distinction from the Father and the Son? Considerations would need to be given to the role of the Holy Spirit at the baptism of Jesus, for example, or the role attributed to the Holy Spirit in the Great Commission, such as when Jesus commanded the disciples to go into all the world and make disciples, baptizing them *in the name of the Father, Son, and Holy Spirit* (Matt. 28:19). Similar weight would need to be given to the meaning of the blasphemy against the Holy Spirit (Luke 12:10), and why such a thing would be deemed unforgiveable!

There are also those extraordinary words of our Lord in the Upper Room in John 14–16, speaking of the Holy Spirit almost as His personal representative agent: "I go away, and come again unto you" (John 14:28). He is speaking about the Holy Spirit whom He describes as a *paraklete*, a *parakletos*, an advocate, a counselor, someone who will speak on His behalf. There is the intercession of the Spirit in Romans 8, and the grieving of the Spirit in Ephesians 4, and the sealing of the Spirit in Ephesians 3.

The Holy Spirit is understood in the New Testament as God—as much God as the Son is God; as much God as the Father is God. Three persons, three distinctions within the unity of God. God is thus One in essence, three in persons. The three persons are one in unity of essence.

As the church Fathers thought through the evidence and data of the New Testament to formulate some kind of doctrine, two key issues surfaced. The first was the phrase *opera ad extra trinitatus indivisa sum*—"the external operations of the Trinity cannot be divided." There is no part of God's work outside of Himself that does not function in Trinitarian terms. Creation, redemption, and judgment involve all three persons of the Godhead. It is the work of the Father, the Son, and the Holy Spirit. And yet, at the same time, the church fathers said there is something that complements that. They called it the *doctrine of appropriation*—that each person of the Trinity appropriates to Himself an aspect of that external operation. It is the Father who predestines; it is the Son who accomplishes; it is the Spirit who applies. While each person of the Trinity communes with each other as One—what the Latin church called *circumincessio,* and the Greek church called *perichoresis*—each individual person appropriates a particular aspect of the work.

We have, of course, merely begun to unravel the incomprehensible. It may be said of the doctrine of the Trinity as has been said of the book of Job, "Scripture is like a river...broad and deep, shallow enough here for the lamb to go wading, but deep enough there for the elephant to swim."[9]

---

9. Gregory the Great, *Moralia,* section 4.

# CHAPTER 2

# Under the Sun to Beyond the Sun: The Old Testament's Worldview

*Michael Barrett*

There is hardly another book of the Bible more maligned, misunderstood, and ignored than the book of Ecclesiastes. Words like *pessimistic, fatalistic, skeptical, cynical, materialistic* often describe how so many perceive the book. The easy solution to this negative perception has been to declare the book to be nothing more than the product of man's reasoning apart from revelation. The purpose of the book, if that be true, is therefore to record for us the kind of life and mindset that is to be avoided rather than regarding it as every other book of the Bible whose inspiration guarantees its consequent profitability for doctrine, reproof, correction, and instruction in righteousness. Without question the book has many surface problems that must be resolved and explained in the light of the specific contexts and overall message and intent of the book.

One of the things that helps remove the stigma associated with Ecclesiastes is a proper understanding of some of the repetitive words and expressions that occur so frequently in the book. So before I address the topic at hand, it will be profitable to define some of the key expressions. At the top of the list are the many references to vanity. The book begins, "Vanity of vanities, saith the Preacher, vanity of vanities; all is vanity" (1:2). After all is said and done, the Preacher says, "Vanity of vanities…all is vanity" (12:8). The term *vanity* occurs at least thirty times throughout the book, giving the impression indeed that all is vanity. One might expect the assessment that life without God is vain, but the conclusion is that even when God is factored in, everything is vain. The Hebrew idiom of linking a singular noun to its own plural is a way of expressing a superlative idea (like King of kings, Holy of Holies, etc.): this is extreme vanity, suggesting we just say, "What's the use?" However, the word translated *vanity* actually means *breath* and is used as a live metaphor to describe a number of things identified specifically in context. When interpreting metaphors, we must identify the topic (what is being talked about), the image (the illustration of what is being talked about), and the point of similarity (what is true about the image that is like what is being talked about). In a live metaphor, the point of similarity between the topic and the image can vary and must be determined from the context in which it occurs. What is true about breath that applies to life or some specific element of it? The most common points of similarity will be either that which is unsubstantial or that which is temporary. Breath is a vapor that is here and then gone as visibly evident on a cold winter day. It does not suggest the idea of uselessness; on the contrary, breath is most necessary. The fact that the stuff and experiences of life are temporary is not necessarily a pessimistic assessment, just a statement of reality. Recognizing the brevity of life is a key component in a proper philosophy of life or worldview.

Breath is the most common, but there are a few more expressions that require definition to keep things in perspective. The phrase "under the sun" occurs almost thirty times and refers to the sphere of physical life. It is where we live and experience life; it is where we can employ our senses. The axiom "vexation of spirit" only occurs seven times, but that is enough to cast a cloud. Literally, this is "striving for or chasing after wind." Rather than referring to the depression of soul, it refers to the futility of a particular action; it is impossible to catch the wind. Finally, the injunction to eat, drink, and enjoy does not advise hedonism, but rather contentment and full use of what God has given to sustain life. It involves the recognition that all that we have in life is God's provision and we should use it with satisfaction. Or in Pauline terms, "for I have learned, in whatsoever state I am, therewith to be content" (Phil. 4:11).

In the face of all the negativity leveled against Ecclesiastes, it is crucial to remember that its message had its origin in the One Great Shepherd, the Lord God Himself, who graciously revealed His upright and true words (12:10, 11) to the Preacher (Qoheleth) for man's good. This book declares the philosophy of life, the worldview, that ought to govern the life of every believer and attract every sinner to the Lord; it is a theology of life that is marked by fearing and obeying God and designed to give contentment during life and certain hope for the afterlife. Unless man, whether saint or sinner, understands and implements this message, the real meaning and purpose of life will remain a mystery, and frustration and despair will rule. To seek satisfaction and contentment in the things of life is to look in the wrong place. The message of Ecclesiastes constantly points to the eternal God who only can satisfy man and requires that the "stuff" of time be evaluated and used in light of the certain reality of eternity.

Ecclesiastes 3:11–14 is the key passage that states the premise for this God-centered view of the world and life:

> He hath made every thing beautiful in his time: also he hath set the world in their heart, so that no man can find out the work that God maketh from the beginning to the end. I know that there is no good in them, but for a man to rejoice, and to do good in his life. And also that every man should eat and drink, and enjoy the good of all his labour, it is the gift of God. I know that, whatsoever God doeth, it shall be for ever: nothing can be put to it, nor any thing taken from it: and God doeth it, that men should fear before him.

That God has made everything beautiful means that He has made everything right or appropriate in its time. This equates to Romans 8:28 which declares that God is working everything to good. Life does not happen haphazardly by blind fate but according to God's all-wise plan. God's setting the world in the heart is a crucial point. Almost everywhere else, the Hebrew word translated *world* refers to eternity. This is a key to understanding why the temporal things of life under the sun cannot ultimately satisfy. Although every man is mortal under the sun, he will live someplace forever. There is, for certain, a life beyond the sun. The only source of satisfaction for the eternity within us is the eternal God. That man can't find things out now means that notwithstanding how beautiful God's plan is, it is incomprehensible to us. The appropriate way to respond to God's unchangeable plan is to not deny it nor rebel against it, but rather to fear God and enjoy life with full contentment in the will of God.

A biblical philosophy of life or worldview must link life to God. How we view the Lord determines how we view life. How we view life is a mirror of how we view the Lord. Recognizing and submitting to the Lord God is essential to a biblical philosophy of life. Living under the sun requires looking beyond the sun. That sums up the Old Testament's worldview and it should ours as well. Qoheleth draws attention to four key truths about God and their implications in establishing a theology for life.

## God Is the Powerful Creator

Throughout Scripture God's creating work testifies to His infinite power, wisdom, and glory. Only God has the power and ability to create, and all that He has created in one way or another testifies to and reveals His awesome glory. There is hardly a more foundational theological truth than the fact that God is the Creator. The inescapable implication of this basic truth is that God, therefore, owns everything, including us. To admit that we belong to the Lord by virtue of His creating us will impact our understanding and experience of life. Qoheleth's orthodox declaration of God the Creator is threefold.

First, He made everything. In 11:5 Qoheleth describes God as the one who made all. In 3:11, the theme verse of the book, he explicitly declares that God has made everything beautiful. The language is all-inclusive; God made the totality. Whatever exists, God has made by Himself, for Himself, for His pleasure and glory (cf. Col. 1:16–17). The vastness, complexities, and details of the creation are ultimately incomprehensible to man, and that itself ought to draw man to that One who is infinitely superior. Everything in this world belongs to the Creator, and there is no possibility of ultimately understanding anything apart from God. To believe that this world is the result of some chance and random evolution of chaos to order is to wander blindly and aimlessly, stumbling to nowhere. There should be little wonder that so many in this world are in constant despair as they vainly search for the meaning of life while denying that God is the Creator. On the other hand, to believe that this world is the work of an all-wise, powerful Creator gives the foundation of reason and logic to all that is, even when the reason for things remains hidden to us. Faith knows there is reason because there is a Creator.

Second, He made man. The Genesis account of the original creation reveals that although man shares much in common with other created life forms, he is unique in that he is made in the image of God; man marks the apex of God's creating work. Man is a spiritual, ultimately immortal being with intellect, emotion, and will, created in original righteousness, holiness, and knowledge, with dominion over the rest of creation. A proper philosophy of life must recognize that man is personally accountable to the Creator and that man's unique place in this world is due not to the struggling of the species to survive, but to the design of God. Qoheleth echoes Genesis. After lamenting the deplorable state of humanity in general (7:25–28), Qoheleth acknowledges that "God hath made man upright" (7:29). The word *upright* refers to man's ethical, not physical, posture. It speaks of man's original state of innocence, including that straight and righteous status before the Lord. Qoheleth seems to understand by this word the pre-fall nature of that divine image: righteousness, true holiness, and knowledge (cf. Eph. 4:24; Col. 3:10). The Preacher also acknowledges the uniqueness of man from the rest of creation when declaring that God set eternity in man's heart (3:11). There is something about man that will live forever and cannot, therefore, be satisfied with temporal things. The tragedy is that in spite of what God made man, man by his sin rejects the knowledge of God, loses his righteousness, and gives himself to the pursuit of his own schemes and plans (7:29b). It is part of sin to ignore the Creator. Qoheleth's investigation of life and experience revealed that the more man follows his own imagination in trying to find meaning, purpose, and satisfaction in life, the further he removes himself from the Lord, and the more desperate life becomes. That man denies his accountability and responsibility to the Creator does not abrogate that duty; it only jeopardizes his immortal soul. What the Preacher observed in his generation is certainly true in ours: there is nothing new under the sun.

Third, He made me. The doctrine of creation, like all doctrine, must be personalized if it is to have practical influence in daily living. In his closing argument, Qoheleth issues the imperative, "remember now thy Creator" (12:1). Remembering is an act of the will. It means to consciously bring something to mind, to make oneself think about something on purpose. A Christian philosophy of life requires that every believer bring to bear on the issues of life the fact that God made him. The implications of this personalized truth are far reaching. We must be satisfied that God has made us as so pleased Him. Our existence is not an accident, nor just a biological phenomenon. We are, each one, "fearfully and wonderfully made" (Ps. 139:14). When God made us according to His pleasure, He did a good job. We should not question or fret over how He made us. We are accountable to God for what He has made us, not for what He has not made us. Too many Christians tend to compare themselves with others and wish they were different. Because they are not different, they feel sorry for themselves. Whether we are short or tall, black or white, smart or dumb, athletic or clumsy, musical or not, we are what He made us to be. What lesser of God's creation ever complains or feels sorry for itself because it is not something else? If every other facet of creation constantly declares God's glory (Ps. 19), how much more should we!

## God Is the Wise Sovereign

The next life-affecting truth is that God is the all-wise Sovereign and, therefore, He preserves and rules us. Providence is the constant and ordinary work of God whereby He preserves and governs His creation to the designed end of His glory. Included in that glory is the ultimate good of God's people. Belief in the sovereign providence of God is the very opposite of fatalism. The affairs of life do not happen by blind chance; they happen as they are orchestrated in perfect harmony by an all-wise God who both knows and determines the end from the beginning. Qoheleth declares that "the righteous, and the wise, and their works, are in the hand of God" (9:1). Not only are the affairs of life in God's hand, His purposes are secure and unchangeable: "I know that, whatsoever God doeth, it shall be for ever: nothing can be put to it, nor any thing taken from it: and God doeth it, that men should fear before him" (3:14). Living in the constant awareness of God (i.e., fearing Him) puts a spiritual slant on things that is essential to a biblical philosophy of life. Providence assures us that there is a reason for everything, even though that reason may be hidden from our understanding. Faith lays hold of God and dispels the despair that so frequently grips us when we consider life apart from God. Three summary statements personalize Ecclesiastes's teaching concerning this important truth.

First, God determines my times. Believing that God determines our times means that there is no better time for us to live than now. Qoheleth warns against the folly of longing for the "good old days"

(7:10); there is no such thing. Learn lessons from the past and prepare for the future, but live now. The best way to live now is by faith in the all-wise Sovereign. Ecclesiastes 3:1–8, 11 is a vital text. There is a time and purpose for everything that happens. In verses 1–8, Qoheleth employs literary genius to substantiate his conclusion in verse 11 that God has made everything appropriate in its time. A series of fourteen pairs of twenty-eight specific times that have been purposed give the overall impression that in the will of God there is a time for absolutely everything. All the occasions of life are part of the divine order. The twenty-eight specific times mentioned are a sort of brachylogy (a condensed expression or random list to designate the totality of an idea) and include, therefore, all kinds of time. The fourteen pairs are expressed as merismus (the linking of opposite terms to designate totality). For example, "a time to be born, and a time to die" identify not only the moments of birth and death, but encompass all the moments in between.

Although the language intends to convey the idea of inclusiveness, the particular times mentioned are instructive. Throughout this list of times are important lessons. A practical belief in the sovereignty of God (that He determines the times of life) will enable us to live through the vicissitudes of life with confidence and good sense. Good sense always accompanies good theology. For instance, weeping and mourning are among the times of life ordained as appropriate (3:4). Trusting the sovereignty of God does not demand a stoic response to tragedy. Stoicism is not faith. Faith weeps in weeping times while resting contentedly in the Lord's always good will. Not sorrowing as the world sorrows does not mean not sorrowing at all. We must learn to trust and pray that God will enable us to use and experience all our times to His glory.

Second, He determines my circumstances. One of the common themes in Ecclesiastes is that God has given us our lot or portion in life. A proper philosophy of life requires contentment and satisfaction with what He has given us. Discontentment usually comes when we pout over what we do not have in comparison with someone else. Over and again Qoheleth identifies the many gifts God has given His people for their good. For example, He has given us our families. In 9:9 he issues the imperative to "live joyfully with the wife whom thou lovest…which he hath given thee…for that is thy portion in this life." What the Authorized Version translates *live joyfully* literally means *see life*. To see life is to experience life. God has made man to be a social being, and the bedrock of society and social relationships is the family, the foundation of which is the union between husband and wife. By logical extension this includes not just the marriage relationship, but the whole family structure as one of the great treasures of life from the Lord. It does not take much experience in living to realize how important the family is to the whole welfare of society. If we do not delight in the families God has given us, there is little chance that we can know contentment in anything else. A good home with a good relationship between husband and wife can erase a lot of the mundane cares of life. Enjoying the family that the Lord has ordained is a key element in a God-centered philosophy of life. Qoheleth's theology here parallels Moses's when he compares a family life that operates with constant reference to the Lord to "days of heaven upon the earth" (Deut. 11:21).

Another key example of divinely determined circumstance concerns our vocations. This along with family probably encompasses more of daily life than anything else. God has given us our labor and the ability to enjoy it (2:10, 24; 3:13; 5:18); therefore, we should work diligently to His glory (9:10). It is tragic that so many people, even Christians, hate what they have to do to make a living. Granted, there is a curse associated with labor, but labor itself is not the curse. Not only is labor a practical means of providing the essentials of life, it is a means of occupying the times of life. Idleness serves no good purpose. The profit of labor is not in what is left over, but in taking full advantage of the experience. The profitability of labor is not to be judged by what pays the most or makes the most contribution to humanity; all that is vanity and will soon fade as vapor.

To acknowledge that even the most ordinary work is God's providential gift will encourage faithful and diligent operation of that labor to the glory of God. For a Christian there is no labor more important than what God has given. Whether in the pulpit, in the factory, or in the home, God-given labor ought to be a source of contentment and pleasure in this temporary world. This is a vital truth for God's people. So often believers hear on the Lord's Day that they should give themselves in total dedication to the Lord's service, and they desperately want to do that. After all, there is only one life and that will soon pass and it's only what's done for Christ that will last. But after Sunday comes Monday with all the mundane affairs necessary for daily survival. How can working on the assembly line making Chevys or Fords have any lasting value? Depression sets in until Sunday starts the cycle again. But even making Chevys is God's gift designed for good.

Third, He determines everything for my good. This is the bottom line. A Christian philosophy of life trusts the Lord that He knows and does what is best for His people. That the Lord regards His people as special and treats them differently than sinners is a glorious truth of the gospel. Qoheleth believed, like Paul, that all things work together for good to those who love God. According to Qoheleth, whereas God gives the sinner travail, He gives the man who is good before Him wisdom, knowledge, and joy (2:26): the skill to live and the capacity to be content. But whatever the particular manifestations of God's governing our times and circumstances (whether "good" times or "bad"), His purpose is to bring us to greater faith and dependence on Him. Ecclesiastes 7:14 says it all. God juxtaposes the good days and bad days for the purpose of bringing us to the end of ourselves and finding complete satisfaction in the Lord Himself. Whenever God's people come to depend on Him completely, that is their good. It is good and comforting to know that "the righteous, and the wise, and their works, are in the hand of God" (9:1).

## God Is the Infallible Judge

Throughout the experience of God's people in every generation, the anomalies of justice and apparent inequities of life have been a test to faith and potential hindrance to a proper view of life itself. It was part of Qoheleth's observation of life that wickedness was in the place of judgment and iniquity was in the place of righteousness (3: 16). That God is the infallible Judge of every man assures that justice will prevail. Indeed, the doctrine of the final judgment ought to be a deterrent to sin as well as a source of consolation for the godly in times of adversity because it guarantees that all will be well in the end. Qoheleth emphasizes two essential truths concerning God's judgment.

First, His judgment is absolutely comprehensive. The final word of the book is that "God shall bring every work into judgment, with every secret thing, whether it be good, or whether it be evil" (12:14). Based on infinite knowledge, God's judgment will make no mistakes and, therefore, no excuses will provide defense in that day. To know that He knows ought to stop us short of sin, guard us in temptations, and guide us to holiness. To live in the reality that "all things are naked and opened unto the eyes of him with whom we have to do" (Heb. 4:13) ought to be an incentive to purity throughout the course of our lives.

Second, His judgment is certain. Qoheleth's theology equals the New Testament: "it is appointed unto men once to die, but after this the judgment" (Heb. 9:27). A main thrust of Qoheleth's teaching is to live with the "after this" in mind. In 11:9–10 he encourages the young man to rejoice and take full advantage of life, but with a view to the certainty that "for all these things God will bring thee into judgment." He then makes the appropriate application to remove irritation from the heart and put away evil from the flesh: in other words, to be content with the life God has given and to strive to be holy. A proper philosophy of life requires living with eternity in sight; true happiness and contentment *now* is possible only with a view to *then*. This life is not all there is; in fact, it is only a small portion of what really is. The certainty of judgment, the day of reckoning, is also a guarantee of justice and terror to the ungodly. Qoheleth warns sinners not to interpret the delay of justice to mean that justice will not come: "Though a sinner do evil a hundred times…it shall not be well with the wicked." (8:11–13). The current anomalies of justice that are so common will be set right when "God shall judge the righteous and the wicked" (3:17). This is part of God's unchangeable purpose (3:17).

### God Is the Supreme Reality

Man's inability to know is a prominent theme in Ecclesiastes: whether the "whys" of life or the "whats" of the future (e.g., 6:12; 9:1, 10, 12; 10:14; 11:2, 6). This ignorance can easily produce anxiety, feelings of uncertainty, and questions concerning the ultimate realities and meaning of life. Throughout his investigation, Qoheleth constantly draws away from the things of life as the answer to any of the ultimate questions. After all is said and done, his conclusion is that everything in life is vanity (a breath that is fleeting and unsubstantial) and that the "totality" for man is to fear God and keep His commandments (12:8, 13). Fearing God and obeying God always go together. This is the bottom line for a Christian philosophy of life. Although there are several elements and implications of fearing God, the concept can best be summarized as living in the awareness of God. The more we are aware of the Lord, the better we will live. He is the supreme reality; nothing is more real or absolute than He. Living in the conscious awareness that God is real is more than just jargon or creedal affirmation; it must be the mindset of every believer. The believer must consciously factor in the reality of God to every situation and circumstance of life. Three observations are possible from Qoheleth's attention to the fear of God.

First, fearing God is the secret to trusting Him concerning all the uncertainties of life. The things about life that defy explanation are themselves evidence of the Lord God who made things that way (3:11–14; 8:17). The fact that we cannot understand all or alter His purposes is designed to draw us to Him: "God doeth it, that men should fear before him" (3:14). Faith rests in the reality that He does all well.

Second, fearing God is an aid to worship. Ecclesiastes 5:1–7 establish significant guidelines for proper and spiritual worship of the infinitely superior supreme reality. Verse 7 summarizes the required self-restraint, sincere submission, and spiritual sacrifice with the imperative "fear thou God." Worship is an essential part of Christian living. Conscious awareness of how great God is will generate a worship of reverence, awe, and respect. A true and proper fear of God teaches that worship is service to Him and not entertainment for us.

Third, fearing God is the defense for the judgment. What happens in eternity is infinitely more important than what happens in life. Ecclesiastes 8:12 assures that "it shall be well with them that fear God, which fear before him." This fear must be understood in its full theological and evangelical significance. To fear God is to know Him as He reveals Himself. The same Preacher said "the fear of the LORD is the beginning of knowledge" (Prov. 1:7) and "the fear of the LORD is the beginning of wisdom: and the knowledge of the holy is understanding" (Prov. 9:10). In the Old Testament, fearing God is the essence of spiritual religion and a vital relationship to the Lord. It is the beginning, the middle, and the end of true life; it is the only thing that will do a man good in life and better in death. To see the final and full significance requires the definition of spiritual knowledge given by Jesus Christ: "This is life eternal, that they may know thee the only true God, and Jesus Christ, whom thou hast sent (John 17:3). It is impossible to know God, the supreme reality, without knowing Jesus Christ. It is only by knowing Christ as Savior that there will be salvation on the day of judgment. That has always been true. Therefore, this book that is so concerned with dealing with the issues of living finds its ultimate solution in forcing men to consider God and His gracious provisions for both this life and the life to come.

We now live under the sun. But this life is temporary and will soon pass away. The psalmist described life as nothing more than an overnight lodging (49:12; *abideth* means to spend the night). How quickly it passes! The best view of life in this world under the sun is to look to that life beyond the sun. That's the Old Testament's worldview. Or as Jonathan Edwards famously put it: live with eternity stamped on your eyelids.

# CHAPTER 3

# The Worldview of
# the Puritans

*Joel R. Beeke and Paul M. Smalley*

The Puritans did not use the term *worldview*, for such terminology did not appear until the late eighteenth century in Germany and was popularized in the nineteenth century.[1] But the Puritans still had a worldview, which was shaped by the written Word of God. With this divinely given worldview they could examine themselves and the world they lived in. They also had a burning passion to pass on this scriptural worldview to their congregations by teaching them "all the counsel of God" (Acts 20:27), which Matthew Poole (1624–1670) understood to be "the whole doctrine of Christianity, as it directs to a holy life."[2] The Puritans were missionaries to people in their homeland of the British Isles; they understood that it is not enough to just paste Christian language and ritual on top of a fundamentally pagan perspective. As the early Puritans surveyed the towns and countryside of England in the 1560s and 1570s, they realized, as J. I. Packer wrote, "The religion of justification by faith was as little known, and superstition was as widespread and deep-rooted, as it had been for the previous century" before the Reformation had come.[3] They responded with a massive effort to shape the beliefs, experiences, and practices of people through the ministry of the Word.

If we set out to discuss the whole Puritan worldview, then we would have to teach the equivalent of a class on the Westminster

---

1. "The German word *Weltanschauung* was introduced by Immanuel Kant (1724–1804) and used by writers such as Kierkegaard, Engels, and Dilthey as they reflected on Western culture." Hiebert, *Transforming Worldviews*, 13.

2. Matthew Poole, *Annotations upon the Holy Bible* (New York: Robert Carter and Brothers, 1853), 3:452.

3. J. I. Packer, *A Quest for Godliness: The Puritan Vision of the Christian Life* (Wheaton, Ill.: Crossway, 1990), 52.

Standards. The great truths enunciated by other speakers at this conference, such as a pilgrim mindset, the Trinity, daily godliness, an embrace of the whole Bible, Old Testament and New, and the divine purpose in human suffering, were all affirmed by the Puritans and pervaded their preaching and living. My aim must be more modest. To allow you to see the world through Puritan eyes, we will first talk about one great truth that illuminated the Puritan worldview—God's sovereignty (especially His fatherly sovereignty), and then how the Puritans viewed several major areas of life through this lens.

## A Worldview Illuminated by God's Sovereignty

The worldview of the Puritans was God-centered. They taught that creation and providence are the work of God in execution of His eternal decrees. As the Westminster Larger Catechism (Q. 15) affirms: "God did in the beginning, by the word of his power, make of nothing the world, and all things therein, for himself, within the space of six days, and all very good." The Larger Catechism establishes God's claim on the world and all who dwell in it. History is the unfolding of His will for us and the record of our response to it, for better or worse. Nor has the God of the Bible left us to our own devices. The Larger Catechism (Q. 18) states, "God's works of providence are his most holy, wise, and powerful preserving and governing all his creatures; ordering them, and all their actions, to his own glory."[4] Thus the worldview of the Puritans revolved around the sovereignty exercised by God as "Maker of heaven and earth" and "the supreme Lord and King of all the world" (Apostles' Creed, Art. 1; Westminster Confession of Faith, 23.1).

*Reformation Roots of the Puritan Worldview*

The Puritans based their view of reality upon God's fatherly sovereignty because they received this biblical heritage from their forefathers, the Reformers of the sixteenth century. John Calvin (1509–1564) understood that the foundation of all our wisdom is the knowledge of God. He wrote: "It will not suffice simply to hold that there is one whom all ought to honor and adore, unless we are also persuaded that he is the fountain of every good, and that we must

---

4. James Dennison, ed., *Reformed Confessions* (Grand Rapids: Reformation Heritage Books, 2014), 4:302.

seek nothing elsewhere than in him." Calvin said, "No drop will be found either of wisdom and light, or of righteousness or power or rectitude, or of genuine truth, which does not flow from him, and of which he is not the cause." Calvin concluded, "I call 'piety' that reverence joined with love for God which the knowledge of his benefits induces. For until men recognize that they owe everything to God, that they are nourished by his fatherly care...they will never yield him willing service."[5]

The Heidelberg Catechism (Q. 1) says much of the Christian's comfort is due to the assurance that "without the will of my heavenly Father, not a hair can fall from my head."[6] The universal sovereignty of God is thus intensely personal for the believer who rejoices in his new status as the adopted child of God. The catechism affirms this in Question 26:

> The eternal Father of our Lord Jesus Christ (who of nothing made heaven and earth, with all that is in them; who likewise upholds and governs the same by His eternal counsel and providence) is for the sake of Christ His Son, my God and my Father; on whom I rely so entirely, that I have no doubt but He will provide me with all things necessary for soul and body; and further, that He will make whatever evils He sends upon me, in this valley of tears, turn out to my advantage; for He is able to do it, being Almighty God, and willing, being a faithful Father.[7]

The dominant theme of the Reformed worldview, which is the very "marrow of Calvinism," is that as the sovereign Creator, Sustainer, and Governor of all things, God reigns through His Son Jesus Christ by the Holy Spirit. B. B. Warfield (1851–1921) rightly said, "The Calvinist, in a word, is the man who sees God.... God in nature, God in history, God in grace. Everywhere he sees God in His mighty stepping, everywhere he feels the working of His mighty arm, the throbbing of His mighty heart."[8]

---

5. John Calvin, *Institutes of the Christian Religion*, ed. John T. McNeill, trans. Ford Lewis Battles (Philadelphia: Westminster, 1960), 1.2.1.

6. *The Three Forms of Unity* (Birmingham, Ala.: Solid Ground Christian Books, 2010), 68.

7. *The Three Forms of Unity*, 75–76.

8. Benjamin B. Warfield, *Calvin as a Theologian and Calvinism Today* (London: Evangelical Press, 1969), 27.

*The Puritan Hope in God's Sovereignty*

The Puritans viewed the Reformed doctrine of God's sovereignty throughout the Holy Scriptures, and embraced it from the heart. They rejoiced to find in Romans 11:36 a reference point from which they could properly view all things: "For of him, and through him, and to him, are all things: to whom be glory for ever. Amen." William Ames (1576–1633) concluded that nothing happens according to blind fate, or by mere chance, but that "God has a fixed providence by which He cares for all things and directs them to His own glory."[9]

In this worldview, hope triumphs over experience. The Puritans lived in a dangerous world where plague, fire, and war killed many people before they reached middle age, and many children before they reached adulthood. With eyes of faith the Puritans saw the devil going about like a roaring lion seeking someone to devour. Nonetheless, they took great hope from the sovereignty of their covenant-keeping God and Father in heaven. Obadiah Sedgwick (c. 1600–1658) wrote, "No one is so fit to govern the world as He who made it."[10] This God exercises perfect wisdom, holiness, justice, and power in His government so that He orders the circumstances, fixes the times, and appoints the means to accomplish His goals.[11]

The Puritans clung to the promise of Romans 8:28, "We know that all things work together for good to them that love God, to them who are the called according to his purpose." The Puritans did not see this sovereign God as a distant figure but as their loving Father in Jesus Christ, so that in all of life they "are pitied, protected, provided for, and chastened by Him as by a Father: yet never cast off," as the Westminster Confession of Faith (Art. 12) affirms.[12] Thomas Watson (c. 1620–1686) wrote, "All the various dealings of God with his children do by a special providence turn to their good. 'All the paths of the Lord are mercy and truth unto such as keep his covenant'

---

9. William Ames, *A Sketch of the Christian's Catechism*, trans. Todd M. Rester (Grand Rapids: Reformation Heritage Books, 2008), 55. This section is adapted from Joel R. Beeke and Sinclair B. Ferguson, "The Puritans on Providence," in Joel R. Beeke and Mark Jones, *A Puritan Theology: Doctrine for Life* (Grand Rapids: Reformation Heritage Books, 2012), 163, 173.

10. Obadiah Sedgwick, *Providence Handled Practically*, ed. Joel R. Beeke and Kelly Van Wyck (Grand Rapids: Reformation Heritage Books, 2007), 10.

11. Sedgwick, *Providence Handled Practically*, 14–15.

12. Thomas Watson, *All Things for Good* (1663; repr., Edinburgh: Banner of Truth, 2001), 11.

(Ps. 25:10)."[13] He said, "The grand reason why all things work for good, is the near and dear interest which God has in His people. The Lord has made a covenant with them. 'They shall be my people, and I will be their God' (Jer. 32:38)."[14]

God's providence offers great comfort to His covenant people. Sedgwick said, "No good man ever lacked anything that was good for him. I may lack a thing which is good, but not which is good for me: 'For the LORD God is a sun and shield: the LORD will give grace and glory: no good thing will he withhold from them that walk uprightly' (Ps. 84:11)."[15] God has a special providence over His church because we are the apple of His eye, His little children, His lambs, and His jewels (Zech. 2:8; Isa. 40:11; 49:15; Mal. 3:17).[16] His care for His people is gracious, compassionate, mysterious, glorious, exact, and often extraordinary.[17] John Cotton (1584–1652) exclaimed, "Is it a light matter for the God of heaven and earth to be called your Father, since you are but men?" As our Father, God will surely give each Christian "provision for a son here, provision for an heir hereafter," for "God nurtures us" and "hath given us an inheritance."[18]

The Puritan view of God's sovereignty was sweetened by the gospel of grace. Their perspective on life was both serious and joyful because the Lord of all things is the Father of Jesus Christ, through whose atoning blood believers become children of God. As obedient children led by God's Word and Spirit, Christians then live to please and honor their Holy Father with the hope that His kingdom is coming.[19] The Puritans aspired to walk with this God, experiencing distinct communion with the Father, the Son, and the Holy Spirit (cf. 2 Cor. 13:14).[20]

---

13. Watson, *All Things for Good*, 11.

14. Watson, *All Things for Good*, 52.

15. Sedgwick, *Providence Handled Practically*, 18.

16. Sedgwick, *Providence Handled Practically*, 21–22.

17. Sedgwick, *Providence Handled Practically*, 29–30.

18. John Cotton, *A Practical Commentary, Or an Exposition With Observations, Reasons, and Uses upon the First Epistle General of John* (London: by R. I. and E. C. for Thomas Parkhurst, 1656), 218 (on 1 John 3:1).

19. See Joel R. Beeke, *Heirs with Christ: The Puritans on Adoption* (Grand Rapids: Reformation Heritage Books, 2008).

20. John Owen, *Of Communion with God the Father, Son, and Holy Ghost*, in *The Works of John Owen* (Edinburgh: Banner of Truth, 1965), vol. 2.

## A Christian Worldview Applied to Every Area of Life

The universal scope of God's sovereignty teaches us that we must glorify Him with all of our being. There is no "must" to enjoying God; it is but the consequence of glorifying Him. Do the one, and you will have the other. The Puritans fervently practiced this conviction in seeking to bring all of life under the direction of God's Word. They believed in the great conclusion of Ecclesiastes 12:13: "Fear God, and keep his commandments: for this is the whole duty of man." John Bunyan (1628–1688) said that fearing God "sanctifies the whole duty of man."[21] He wrote, "It is a universal grace; it will stir up the soul unto all good duties. It is a fruitful grace, from which…flows abundance of excellent virtues, nor without it can there be anything good, or done well that is done."[22]

To be lived out, a worldview must be practical, and that requires wisdom. The Reformation doctrine of justification by faith alone released Christians from an unbiblical system of sacramental salvation and church-mandated penance. After the Reformation, the human tendency to drift into formalism and inconsistency of doctrine and practice became commonplace. The Puritans revived Reformation doctrine and made it more practical by stressing how to live the Christian life in every possible facet. Authors such as Richard Greenham (c. 1542–1594), Richard Rogers (1550–1618), William Perkins (1558–1602), William Ames, and Richard Baxter (1615–1691) wrote treatises addressing various "cases of conscience" to guide believers on how to fear the Lord and do His will in every sphere of human existence.[23]

Since so much is available today on Puritan views of personal godliness, family piety, and church reformation, we will touch briefly on these topics before immersing ourselves in the Puritan views of economics and politics.

*Godly Personal Life*

Ultimately, each of us will stand before the Lord to be judged for our own thoughts, words, and actions in life (2 Cor. 5:10). Therefore, the Puritans placed great emphasis upon personal godliness. The most

---

21. John Bunyan, *Treatise on the Fear of God*, in *The Works of John Bunyan*, ed. George Offor, 3 vols. (1854; repr., Edinburgh: Banner of Truth, 1991), 1:491.

22. Bunyan, *Treatise on the Fear of God*, in *Works*, 1:465.

23. See *A Puritan Theology*, 927–45.

important "case of conscience" they addressed was, "Am I a true child of God?"[24] The Puritans relished full assurance of salvation and peace with God through the blood of Christ, for both afforded the believer the stability and power to serve God. Knowing God as a loving Father through Jesus Christ helped a believer live for God's pleasure by the Holy Spirit as directed through the written Word.

The Puritans believed that all of life should be offered to God as a continual act of consecration in response to His mercies (Rom. 12:1). Henry Scudder (c. 1585–1652) titled his devotional manual, *The Christian's Daily Walk in Holy Security and Peace*, which John Owen judged to be written with "weight and wisdom in the directions given in it for practice…breathing of a spirit of holiness, zeal, humility, and the fear of the Lord."[25] Owen's words summarize the Puritan view of personal godliness lived by faith in Jesus Christ.

### Godly Domestic Life

The Puritans taught that the family is a divine institution; God is the Lord of the home and of all the relationships found in it. They stressed piety as family piety, for they saw the household as the first and fundamental unit of all human society.[26] William Gouge (1575–1653) wrote that "a family is a little church and a little nation," and "a school where the first principles" of society are learned and practiced.[27] As a "little church," the family was the setting of primary religious nurture, and so the Puritans strongly advocated family worship and instruction from a catechism based on the Bible. The Westminster divines intended that their work not only direct pastors and churches, but also that fathers and mothers use the catechisms and confession in the regular instruction of their children, so that

---

24. See Joel R. Beeke, *The Quest for Full Assurance: The Legacy of Calvin and His Successors* (Edinburgh: Banner of Truth, 1999).

25. John Owen, Recommendation, in Henry Scudder, *The Christian's Daily Walk in Holy Security and Peace* (Harrisonburg, Va.: Sprinkle, 1984), 9.

26. The family is "the very first society that by the direction and providence of God, is produced among the children of men." Cotton Mather, *Family Religion Urged* (Boston, 1709), 1, cited in Edmund S. Morgan, *The Puritan Family: Religion and Domestic Relations in Seventeenth-Century New England* (New York: Harper and Row, 1966), 133.

27. William Gouge, *Building a Godly Home, Volume 1, A Holy Vision for Family Life*, ed. Scott Brown and Joel R. Beeke (Grand Rapids: Reformation Heritage Books, 2013), 20.

they might say with Joshua, "As for me and my house, we will serve the LORD" (Josh. 24:15).[28]

The Puritans wrote dozens of treatises about family life, describing the proper roles and relationships between husbands and wives, fathers, mothers, and children.[29] They placed every family relationship in the light of God's sovereignty and fatherhood, and called

28. See the Epistle to the Reader in *Westminster Confession of Faith* (Glasgow: Free Presbyterian Publications, 1994), 5–12.

29. Henry Smith, *A Preparative to Marriage*, in *The Works of Henry Smith* (repr., Staffordshire: Tentmaker Publications, 2002), 1:5–40; William Whately, *A Bride-Bush or A Wedding Sermon* (1617; repr., Norwood, N.J.: Walter J. Johnson, 1975); *A Care-Cloth: Or, the Cumbers and Troubles of Marriage* (1624; repr., Norwood, N.J.: Walter J. Johnson, 1975); Arthur Hildersham, *Dealing with Sin in Our Children*, ed. Don Kistler (Morgan, Pa.: Soli Deo Gloria, 2004); Richard Stock, *A Commentary Upon the Prophecy of Malachi*, 168–91. In *Richard Stock and Samuel Torshell on Malachi and Richard Bernard and Thomas Fuller on Ruth* (1865; repr., Stoke-on-Trent: Tentmaker, 2006); Paul Bayne, *An Entire Commentary upon the Whole Epistle of St. Paul to the Ephesians* (1866; repr., Stoke-on-Trent: Tentmaker, 2001), 337–64; Daniel Rogers, *Matrimonial Honor* (1642; repr., Warrenton, Virginia: Edification Press, 2010); Ames, *Conscience with the Power and Cases Thereof*, 5.21–22, 35–38 (156–59, 196–211); John Davenant, *Colossians*, trans. by Josiah Allport, A Geneva Series Commentary (1831; repr., Edinburgh: Banner of Truth, 2005), 2:151–95; Nicholas Byfield, *An Exposition Upon the Epistle to the Colossians* (1866; repr., Stoke-on-Trent: Tentmaker, 2007), 346–61; William Gouge, *Of Domestical Duties*, ed. Greg Fox (1622; repr., Pensacola: Puritan Reprints, 2006); modernized by Brown and Beeke as *Building a Godly Home* (3 vols.); James Durham, *A Practical Exposition of the Ten Commandments*, ed. Christopher Coldwell (Dallas, Tex.: Naphtali Press, 2002), 221–36; Lewis Stuckley, *A Gospel Glass: Representing the Miscarriages of Professors, Both in Their Personal and Relative Capacities* (1852; repr., Grand Rapids: Ebenezer Publications, 2002), 169–83; Edward Lawrence, *Parent's Concerns for Their Unsaved Children*, ed. Don Kistler (Morgan, Pa.: Soli Deo Gloria, 2003); Baxter, *A Christian Directory*, 2.1–22 (1:394–493); excerpted and published separately as *The Godly Home*, ed. Randall J. Pederson (Wheaton, Ill.: Crossway Books, 2010); George Hamond, *The Case for Family Worship*, ed. Don Kistler (Orlando: Soli Deo Gloria, 2005); Swinnock, *The Christian Man's Calling*, in *Works*, 1:464–528; Richard Adams, "What are the Duties of Parents and Children; and How Are They to Be Managed According to Scripture?" in *Puritan Sermons*, 2:303–358; Thomas Doolittle, "How May the Duty of Daily Family Prayer Be Best Managed for the Spiritual Benefit of Every One in the Family?" in *Puritan Sermons*, 2:194–272; Richard Steele, "What Are the Duties of Husbands and Wives towards Each Other?" in *Puritan Sermons*, 2:272–303; D. B., *An Antidote Against Discord Between Man and Wife* (1685; repr., Warrenton, Virginia: Edification Press, 2013); Matthew Henry, *Family Religion: Principles for Raising a Godly Family* (Ross-shire, Scotland: Christian Focus Publications, 2008); Cotton Mather, *A Family Well-ordered: Or, An Essay to Render Parents and Children Happy in One Another*, ed. Don Kistler (Morgan, Pa.: Soli Deo Gloria, 2001); Thomas Halyburton, "The Christian's Duty, with Respect to Both Personal and Family Religion," in *The Great Concern of Salvation*, in *The Works of Thomas Halyburton* (Aberdeen: James Begg Society, 2000–2003), 2:368–403.

every family member to live in the faith and fear of the Lord. Part of their genius was teaching people to stop looking at what others were doing, and to focus upon what they must do as their loving duty to God. Christ, of course, is the model in this; for what would become of us if Christ treated us the way we treat Him? God's sovereign love is freely given, and so should ours be.

### Godly Ecclesiastical Life

The Puritans varied in their understanding of church polity; some were Episcopalians, some were Congregationalists, and most were Presbyterians. Church government is an important biblical doctrine, but differences on this matter should not obscure the common ground shared by the Puritans in their high ideals concerning pastoral ministry and passionate activism to promote godliness among the people of the church. Packer has argued that "Puritanism was, at its heart, a movement of spiritual revival" in the church, though they did not use the word *revival* so much as *reformation*.[30] They understood that revival is the work of the Spirit, while reformation is also our response to the Word of God.

The Puritans also believed that reformation and revival took place as the Holy Spirit applied the preached word of God. Therefore, they instituted a program for biblical preaching:

- by preaching in a biblical, doctrinal, experiential, and practical manner;
- by establishing lectureships (privately funded preaching ministries) to bring the ministry of the word to parishes lacking a Reformed, experiential pastor;
- by organizing "prophesyings" or conferences where ministers met to hear sermons and discuss good preaching methods while other people listened;
- by publishing their sermons as tracts and books, producing literature full of doctrine and "uses," or applications for all aspects of life; and
- by training preachers at the universities in Cambridge and Oxford to evangelize unreached communities and carry on the ministry in future generations.[31]

---

30. Packer, *A Quest for Godliness*, 37–38.
31. See Joel R. Beeke, "Puritan Preaching (2)," in *A Puritan Theology*, 699–705.

The Puritan approach to revival and reformation reflects their worldview of the supremacy of God above all human authorities. As Perkins said, the faithful preacher is "the voice of God," for he speaks in the name of Christ (2 Cor. 5:19; 2 Thess. 2:13–14), and the Spirit of God speaks through him (1 Cor. 2:4).[32] Since the church is one family with one head under one Father, His Word must prevail in all its beliefs, decisions, and activities.

## Godly Economic Life

The Puritans believed the fear of the sovereign Lord must control the way we conduct our work, finances, and property. Though they gave priority to preaching and the Lord's Day, they saw no division between the sacred and the secular, for they saw all of life as sacred. Hence they sought to glorify God in all that they did. Leland Ryken says, "For the Puritans, all of life was God's. Their goal was to integrate their daily work with their religious devotion to God."[33] This led them to the following economic principles.[34]

### First: Justice in Trade

George Swinnock (c. 1627–1673) said, "True godliness payeth its dues to men, as well as its duty to God.... True holiness will provide things honest [honorable], not only in the sight of God, but also in the sight of men."[35] Swinnock said that Moses came down from Mt. Sinai with two tablets in his hands inscribed with the law that set forth both our duty to God and our duty to our fellow human beings. The Christian who enjoys communion with God shows it by his religion towards God and righteousness towards men.[36] We must deal fairly and justly, or our worship of God is hypocrisy.

---

32. William Perkins, *The Arte of Prophecying*, trans. Thomas Tuke (London: by Felix Kyngston for E. E., 1607), 3, 133.

33. Leland Ryken, *Worldly Saints: The Puritans as They Really Were* (Grand Rapids: Zondervan, 1986), 25.

34. On Puritan economics, see Gary North, "Medieval Economics in Puritan New England, 1630–60," *The Journal of Christian Reconstruction* 5, no. 2 (Winter 1978–1979): 153–93.

35. George Swinnock, *The Christian Man's Calling*, in *The Works of George Swinnock* (Edinburgh: Banner of Truth, 1992), 2:187–88.

36. Swinnock, *The Christian Man's Calling*, in *Works*, 2:189.

Swinnock said we must be careful that our conduct towards other people is consistently "righteous, meek, and courteous."[37] Righteous conduct shows a heart to "deal with men as one that in all hath to do with God." In our buying, selling, and trading, we must focus on what is fair and honest, not seeking to take advantage of people because of their ignorance or desperate situation. We must deliver what we promise, and promise what is true of our goods and services.[38] Baxter said, "He that will glorify his religion and God before men, must be *strictly just in all his dealings*—just in governing, just in trading and bargaining...just in performing all his promises, and in giving every man his right."[39] Swinnock wrote, "In all thy contracts, purchases, and sales, cast an eye upon that golden rule, mentioned by our Saviour, 'Therefore all things whatsoever ye would that men should do to you, do ye even so to them: for this is the law and the prophets' (Matt. 7:12)."[40]

### Second: Faithfulness in Vocation

The Puritan view of economic life embraced the noble idea of divine calling or vocation in society. Perkins said that just as a general assigns each soldier a particular station and duty in his army, so God assigns each person a calling and function in society.[41] Human beings depend on each other like parts of a body. Gouge said, "Our particular places and callings are those bonds that firmly and fitly knit people together, like the members of a natural body by nerves, arteries, sinews, veins, etc., by which life, sense, and motion are communicated from one part to another."[42] This view of each person's place and duty in human society was part of the inheritance the Puritans received from the Reformers.[43]

---

37. Swinnock, *The Christian Man's Calling*, in *Works*, 2:194.

38. Swinnock, *The Christian Man's Calling*, in *Works*, 2:194–200.

39. Baxter, "What Light Must Shine," in *Puritan Sermons*, 2:473, emphasis original, Richard Baxter, "What Light Must Shine in Our Works," in *Puritan Sermons, 1659–1689, Being the Morning Exercises* (Wheaton, Ill.: Richard Owen Roberts, 1981), 2:460.

40. Swinnock, *The Christian Man's Calling*, in *Works*, 2:201.

41. William Perkins, *A Treatise of the Vocations, Or, Callings of Men* (London: John Legat, 1603), 3.

42. Gouge, *Building a Godly Home*, 18–19.

43. For Calvin's view of mutual obligation and cooperation according to our vocations, see Ronald S. Wallace, *Calvin's Doctrine of the Christian Life* (Tyler, Tex.: Geneva Divinity School Press, 1982), 148–56.

The Puritan vision of economics was also about doing as much good as you can, however and whenever you can, for your fellow human beings. Stephen Innes wrote of the New England colonies that their doctrine of vocation "made labor sacred" and built all human endeavor upon a sense of "communal obligation."[44] Cotton Mather (1663–1728) said, "God hath made man a societal creature. We expect benefits from human society. It is but equal that human society should receive benefits from us. We are beneficial to human society by the works of that special occupation in which we are to be employed, according to the order of God."[45]

The Puritan concept of vocation is much bigger than earning money; it includes relationships of authority and submission between civil magistrates and their subjects, ecclesiastical office bearers and church members, heads of households and children, masters and servants or employees.[46] Even if you are wealthy and do not need to work, Perkins said, "Every one, rich or poor, man or woman, is bound to have a personal calling, in which they must perform some duties for the common good, according to the measure of the gifts that God hath bestowed on them."[47]

Fulfilling our daily vocations in the world is the primary way we serve God. Richard Steele (1629–1689) wrote, "God doth call every man and woman, as if he called them by name, to serve him in some peculiar [particular] employment in this world, both for their own and the common good."[48] Steele offered detailed advice about choosing a calling, entering a field of work, and pursuing a trade with wisdom, diligence, fairness, truthfulness, contentment, and devotion to God until He discharges us from our work by a mental or physical disability.[49] The Puritans valued stability in vocation as opposed to frequent job changes. Having a particular calling is very helpful, Baxter said, for it permits you to find more steady work, develop your skills in

---

44. Stephen Innes, *Creating the Commonwealth: The Economic Culture of Puritan New England* (New York: W. W. Norton and Co., 1995), 7.

45. Cotton Mather, *A Christian at His Calling*, cited in Ryken, *Worldly Saints*, 31.

46. Perkins, *A Treatise of the Vocations*, 13, 22–23.

47. Perkins, *A Treatise of the Vocations*, 28.

48. Richard Steele, *The Tradesman's Calling* (London: for J. D. by Samuel Spring, 1684), 1.

49. An abridged version of this book was published, Richard Steele, *The Religious Tradesman* (Trenton: Francis S. Wiggins, 1823), which is available in reprint, print-on-demand, or electronically.

a particular field, and accumulate tools and equipment.[50] All in all, faithfulness in the performance of one's calling brings many benefits in this world, and by God's grace, heavenly treasure in the life to come.

### Third: Stewardship of Resources

The Puritans neither idealized poverty nor wealth—they viewed money as good, but not as their God.[51] Under God, they were stewards of all He entrusted to them. They saw no contradiction between serving God and lawfully making as much money as a calling allows, if you first sought the kingdom of God and the good of your soul. Baxter said, "You may labour in that manner that tendeth most to your success and lawful gain: you are bound to improve [make good use of] all your Master's talents; but then your end must be, that you may be the better provided to do God service, and may do the more good with what you have."[52]

The Puritans taught that good stewardship requires not only hard work and skill in work, but also avoiding wasting resources on foolish diversions and unnecessary expenditures. Ames commended "the virtue of spending only what is worthy and necessary."[53] Baxter said, "Necessary frugality or sparing is an act of fidelity, obedience, and gratitude, by which we use all our estates so faithfully for the chief Owner, so obediently to our chief Ruler, and so gratefully to our chief Benefactor, as that we waste it not any other way."[54] Baxter also warned against wasting money on pampering our bodies or excessive entertainment. The Puritans condemned lack of thrift because it "wastes goods that otherwise could be invested in the good of the civil community," "led to other vices" such as dishonesty and immorality, and, worst of all, was "a fundamental betrayal of both God's priority of ownership and graciousness to human beings."[55] Careless or wasteful living does not use all things for the glory of God.

---

50. Richard Baxter, *A Christian Directory* (Morgan, Pa.: Soli Deo Gloria, 1996), 1.10.1.1.2 (376).

51. See Ryken, *Worldly Saints*, 57–71.

52. Baxter, *A Christian Directory*, 1.10.1 (377).

53. William Ames, *The Marrow of Theology*, trans. John Dykstra Eusden (Grand Rapids: Baker, 1968), 2.20.40 (324). He called this virtue "parsimony."

54. Baxter, *A Christian Directory*, 4.21.1 (851).

55. James Calvin Davis and Charles Mathewes, "Saving Grace and Moral Striving: Thrift in Puritan Theology," in *Thrift and Thriving in America: Capitalism and*

Of course, diligence and thrift tend to generate wealth. For those who grow rich, Perkins offered the following counsel: (1) Let them consider that "God is not only their sovereign Lord, but the Lord of their riches, and they themselves are but the stewards of God, to employ and dispense them, according to his will." (2) Let them cultivate contentment, "so as [they] set not the affection of [their] heart upon [their] riches." (3) Let them be ready to forsake all that they have if God calls them to world missions, if persecutors threaten to take their goods, or if some disaster or war places their community in need of all they have. (4) Let them use and own their goods as will "tend to God's glory, and the salvation of [their] souls" by being "rich in good works."[56]

Though all men are not wealthy, God gives to all a measure of that most valuable of resources: time. The Puritans said much about redeeming the time. Thomas Hooker (1586–1647) wrote, "The life of a Christian is not an idle but a laborious life, that will cost a man much pains and travail, if he will endeavor to be sincere in his profession, and walk uprightly with the Lord in an holy conversation, watching all seasons, and readily embracing all opportunities, as he ought to do, that so whatsoever he doth may tend to God's glory, and to the good of his church and people."[57] By "watching all seasons," he meant recognizing the best use of each hour the Lord gives us so that we may serve both God and men.[58] To that end, Hooker said we "should learn how to cut off all unnecessary expense of time... [and] how to redeem the time out of the hands of our lusts and corruptions."[59] Baxter said, "Remember then that God never gave thee one minute to spend in vain."[60]

The Puritans also valued rest and recreation as wise stewardship of our bodies and minds. They were great defenders of the Christian

*Moral Order from the Puritans to the Present*, ed. Joshua J. Yates and James Davison Hunter (Oxford: Oxford University Press, 2011), 102–103.

56. *William Perkins, 1558–1602, English Puritanist, His Pioneer Works on Casuistry: "A Discourse of Conscience" and "The Whole Treatise of Cases of Conscience,"* ed. Thomas F. Merrill (Nieuwkoop: B. De Graaf, 1966), 192–96. Henceforth cited as Perkins, *Conscience*.

57. Thomas Hooker, *The Saints Guide* (London: John Stafford, 1645), 167–68.

58. Hooker, *The Saints Guide*, 151.

59. Hooker, *The Saints Guide*, 171.

60. Baxter, *A Christian Directory*, 236. See Davis and Mathewes, "Saving Grace and Moral Striving," in *Thrift and Thriving in America*, 106–110.

Sabbath, the weekly day of holy rest, as we see in *The True Doctrine of the Sabbath,* a classic by Nicholas Bownd.[61] They also approved of sports and recreation on the other six days of the week for "the refreshing of body and mind" and for "delight," as Perkins said.[62] He warned, however, that we may not make use of holy things for recreation, nor entertain ourselves with sin or actions tending to sin, or acts of cruelty such as tormenting animals (bear baiting) or forcing creatures to fight each other (cock-fighting). However, Perkins said that it is good to engage in forms of recreation requiring intelligence or skill, such as archery, running, wrestling, or fencing, or board games like chess, checkers (British "draughts"), "the philosopher's game" (or Rithmomachy),[63] or making music. He disapproved of theater, mixed social dancing, games of chance, or gambling for money. He advised that we use recreation in ways that avoid scandal, are for our good and God's glory, refresh mind and body, and do not take up too much of our time or affection, "for we may not set our heart upon sports."[64] Hunting and fishing in England were legally restricted to the noblemen, but when the Puritans crossed the Atlantic they found open forests full of game and especially delighted in fishing.[65] Thus the Puritans delighted in God's creation, seeking rest and refreshment in worthwhile and creative ways.

In the Puritan worldview, godly economics revolve around the goodness of the Creator whose image we bear. They firmly believed Paul's teaching in 1 Timothy 4:4–5, "Every creature of God is good, and nothing to be refused, if it be received with thanksgiving: for it is sanctified by the word of God and prayer." Their economics was also governed by living in such a way that when their Redeemer and Lord returned to judge His servants, they would hear Him graciously say, "Well done, thou good and faithful servant…enter thou into the joy of thy lord" (Matt. 25:21).

---

61. Nicholas Bownd, *Sabbathum Veteris et Novi Testamenti: or, The True Doctrine of the Sabbath*, ed. Chris Coldwell (Grand Rapids: Reformation Heritage Books; Dallas: Naphtali Press, 2015).

62. Perkins, *Conscience,* 217.

63. "Battle of the Numbers," an ancient board game, much like chess, in which the playing pieces have geometric shapes and numerical values.

64. Perkins, *Conscience,* 217–22.

65. Bruce C. Daniels, *Puritans at Play: Leisure and Recreation in Colonial New England*, Tenth Anniversary Edition (New York: Palgrave Macmillan, 1995), 164, 168–71.

**Godly Political Life**

The Puritans lived in an age of political ferment and revolution. In this they embraced the political views derived from Augustine (354–430), the medieval church (especially the conciliar movement), and Reformed theologians[66] such as Calvin,[67] Theodore Beza (1519–1605),[68] and Johannes Althusius (1557–1638).[69] Though this is a complex subject, we may observe seven principles of Puritan political doctrine.

*First: Benevolent Government*

The Puritans believed government is a divine institution. As the Westminster Confession says, "God, the supreme Lord and King of all the world, hath ordained civil magistrates, to be under Him, over the people, for His own glory, and the public good" (23.1). Following the teachings of the Old Testament and Romans 13, the Puritans asserted the authority of the civil magistracy under God, but said it was limited in its power and purpose. Ames wrote, "Ruling is a use of power to further the good of others," citing Roman 13:4, "He is the minister of

---

66. For an introductory survey of the political writings of various sixteenth-century Reformed theologians, see David W. Hall, *Calvin in the Public Square: Liberal Democracies, Rights, and Civil Liberties*, The Calvin 500 Series (Phillipsburg, N.J., P&R, 2009), 129–90.

67. On Calvin's views of government and limited, just war, see Calvin, *Institutes*, 4.20; John T. McNeill, "John Calvin on Civil Government," in *Calvinism and the Political Order*, ed. George L. Hunt (Philadelphia: Westminster, 1965), 23–45; Hall, *Calvin in the Public Square*, 71–104; Paul Marshall, "Calvin, Politics, and Political Science," in *Calvin and Culture: Exploring a Worldview*, ed. David W. Hall and Marvin Padgett, The Calvin 500 Series (Phillipsburg, N.J., P & R, 2010), 142–61; Mark J. Larson, *Calvin's Doctrine of the State: A Reformed Doctrine and Its American Trajectory, The Revolutionary War, and the Founding of the Republic* (Eugene, Ore.: Wipf and Stock, 2009).

68. Theodore Beza, *Du Droit des Magistrats* (1574); translation: *Concerning the Rights of Rulers Over Their Subjects and the Duties of Subjects Toward Their Rulers*, trans. Henri-Louis Gonin (Cape Town and Pretoria, 1956). See Hall, *Calvin in the Public Square*, 158–63.

69. Johannes Althusius was magistrate in Emden and author of *Politica Methodice Digesta* (1603) and *Dicaelogicae* (1617). See Hall, *Calvin in the Public Square*, 173–81; John Witte Jr., "Law, Authority, and Liberty in Early Calvinism," in *Calvin and Culture*, 30–33. For English translations, see *The Politics of Johannes Althusius: An Abridged Translation of the Third Edition of* Politica Methodice Digesta, trans. Frederick S. Carney (Boston: Beacon, 1964); Johannes Althusius, *On Law and Power*, trans. Jeffrey J. Veenstra, intro. Stephen J. Grabill and John Witte, Jr. (Grand Rapids: Christian's Library Press, 2013); previously published without Witte's introduction as "Selections from the Dicaeologicae," *Journal of Markets and Morality* 9, no. 2 (Fall 2006): 399–483.

God to thee for good."[70] The Puritans viewed the state as a "common-wealth," in which a well-ordered community thrives in all its parts.

The office of a magistrate, Ames said, is to give "protection" to good citizens and to execute just laws and judgments. Ames said the magistrate has "the greatest of all human powers," but does not have "absolute" or "unbounded power." A civil ruler must not treat his people like slaves, but he must "show himself as a brother to the rest, and in his function as a father."[71] Samuel Rutherford (1600–1661) said the purpose of government and law is *salus populi*, the safety or well-being of the people, that is, their "quiet and peaceable life in all godliness and honesty" (1 Tim. 2:2).[72] Oliver Cromwell (1599–1658) appealed to the same principle.[73]

*Second: Civil Obedience*
Ames taught that the subjects of a realm owe their magistrate their prayers, honor, obedience, and taxes. The subjects must not be quick to censure their ruler's policies (for they may be ignorant of all the factors involved) and should "tolerate light infirmities and offenses" in their leaders.[74] However, human magistrates are not God, and

---

70. Ames, *The Marrow of Theology*, 2.17.37 (311).

71. William Ames, *Conscience with the Power and Cases Thereof* (Amsterdam, The Netherlands: Theatrum Orbis Terrarum, 1975), 5.15.1–12 (164–65).

72. Samuel Rutherford, *Lex, Rex: The Law and the Prince* (Edinburgh: Robert Ogle and Oliver and Boyd, 1843), Q. 25 (119). On Rutherford's political views, see J. F. Maclear, "Samuel Rutherford: The Law and the King," in *Calvinism and the Political Order*, 65–87; Richard Flinn, "Samuel Rutherford and Puritan Political Theory," *Journal of Christian Reconstruction* 5, no. 2 (Winter 1978–1979): 49–74; Charles E. Rae, "The Political Thought of Samuel Rutherford" (MA thesis, The University of Guelph, 1991); John D. Ford, "*Lex, rex iusto posita*: Samuel Rutherford on the Origins of Government," in *Scots and Britons: Scottish Political Thought and the Union of 1603*, ed. Roger A. Mason (Cambridge: Cambridge University Press, 1994), 262–90; John Coffey, *Politics, Religion and the British Revolutions: The Mind of Samuel Rutherford*, Cambridge Studies in Early Modern British History (Cambridge: Cambridge University Press, 1997); Kingsley G. Rendell, *Samuel Rutherford: A New Biography of the Man and His Ministry* (Ross-shire, Scotland: Christian Focus Publications, 2003), 91–97; David McKay, "Samuel Rutherford on Civil Government," in *Samuel Rutherford: An Introduction to His Theology*, ed. Matthew Vogan (Edinburgh: Scottish Reformation Society, 2012), 253–64. For a review of twentieth-century academic literature on Rutherford, see Coffey, *Politics*, 15–17, 146. For a modern appropriation of Rutherford's views, see Francis A. Schaeffer, *A Christian Manifesto*, rev. ed. (Wheaton, Ill.: Crossway Books, 1982), 99–138.

73. Oliver Cromwell, letter of Nov. 25, 1648, to Col. Robert Hammond, in *Letters and Speeches of Oliver Cromwell*, ed. Thomas Carlyle (London: Methuen, 1904), 1:396.

74. Ames, *Conscience with the Power and Cases Thereof*, 5.15.13–17 (165–66).

"nothing but the law of God doth properly, directly, immediately, and by itself bind the conscience." Subjects obey their magistrate not because of an authority inherent in his person, but because God commands them to do so. Thus "contempt of authority" is "a sin against the law of God." Still, mere human laws have no right to compel us to put our souls in danger by sinning against God, nor should they force us to suffer great injury or shame in earthly concerns merely to please the whim of a tyrant.[75]

### Third: Righteous Legislation

Just laws must be founded upon the laws of God. The Puritans looked to the Old Testament laws for political guidance about how to regulate society. They believed that the moral law expounded in the Ten Commandments forever binds all men and directs civil justice. What about the judicial laws of Israel, together with their prescribed penalties (often death)? Calvin had taught that civil laws should reflect God's moral law,[76] but need not follow the judicial law of Israel with its specific penalties,[77] though Calvin still drew lessons from it, as can be seen in his sermons on Deuteronomy.[78] The Puritans likewise drew wisdom for government from the judicial or case law of Moses, but did not treat it as a binding political system.

Perkins said that some aspects of the judicial law were abrogated with the old dispensation, but others, being rooted in the moral law and serving to guard it like fences, are perpetually binding.[79] Paul Bayne (c. 1573–1617) said that the Mosaic judicial laws apply to us

---

75. Ames, *Conscience with the Power and Cases Thereof*, 5.15.18–24 (166–68).

76. "The office of the magistrates…extends to both tables of the law." Calvin, *Institutes*, 4.20.9.

77. Calvin, *Institutes*, 4.20.14–16.

78. Douglas F. Kelly, *The Emergence of Liberty in the Modern World: The Influence of Calvin on Five Governments from the Sixteenth through Eighteenth Centuries* (Phillipsburg, N.J.: P & R Publishing, 1992), 22. Thus Calvin derived from Deut. 13 the "general rule" that "not only is it lawful for all kings and magistrates to punish heretics and such as have perverted the pure truth, but also that they be bound to do it." John Calvin, *Sermons on Deuteronomy* (1583; repr., Edinburgh: Banner of Truth, 1987), 537.

79. Perkins, *Galatians*, in *Works*, 2:206–209. Thus Perkins taught that the death penalty still pertained to worshipers of false gods, witches, flagrant blasphemers, cursers of parents, murderers, and adulterers. However, he said that modern Christians need not implement the mandatory tithes on agricultural products because other proportion than a tenth might be better, nor punish thieves with fourfold restitution because in Europe it is better to kill them.

now only as instruction in "the perpetual equity of God" in His moral law, but they do not bind us as a political system, nor do they limit us to a particular punishment for a crime.[80] Anthony Burgess (d. 1664) said that the judicial laws are "abrogated," and like the Jewish ceremonial laws, are "made void."[81] Owen exhorted Parliament in 1652 to seek wisdom from the judicial laws, but only insofar as their essential elements may be abstracted from the ancient Jewish national context.[82] Rutherford taught that the judicial law requiring levirate marriage does not bind us at all, and the law condemning a Sabbath-breaker to death teaches us that Sabbath-breakers should be punished, but the punishment need not be death.[83] The Puritan view expressed in the Westminster Confession (19.4) says that Israel's judicial laws "expired" with the end of the Jewish nation, and apply now only in their "general equity" or principles of justice.[84] The Puritans were not "theonomists" in the modern sense of the term, for they did not teach that the judicial laws bind us politically.[85]

*Fourth: Just Warfare*

We must understand the Puritan view of war in its historical context. The expression "just war" comes from Augustine, who referred to wars in general as "slaughter and bloodshed," "great evils," and

---

80. Paul Bayne, *An Entire Commentary on the Whole Epistle of St Paul to the Ephesians* (1866; repr., Stoke-on-Trent, England, Tentmaker, 2007), 162.

81. Anthony Burgess, *Vindiciae Legis: A Vindication of the Morall Law and the Covenants* (1647; repr. Grand Rapids: Reformation Heritage Books, 2011), 211. On Burgess's view of the law in his historical context, see Stephen J. Casselli, *Divine Rule Maintained: Anthony Burgess, Covenant Theology, and the Place of the Law in Reformed Scholasticism*, Studies on the Westminster Assembly (Grand Rapids: Reformation Heritage Books, 2016).

82. Owen, *Christ's Kingdom and the Magistrate's Power*, in *Works*, 8:394.

83. Samuel Rutherford, *A Free Disputation against Pretended Liberty of Conscience* (London: by R. I. for Andrew Crook, 1649), 190.

84. Westminster Confession of Faith (19.4), in *Reformed Confessions*, 4:255; Matthew Winzer, "The Westminster Assembly and the Judicial Law: A Chronological Compilation and Analysis, Part Two: Analysis," in *Confessional Presbyterian* 5 (2009): 56–88. See William Perkins, *Commentary on Galatians*, in *The Works of William Perkins, Volume 2*, ed. Paul M. Smalley (Grand Rapids: Reformation Heritage Books, 2015), 184 (on Gal. 3:13–14); James B. Jordan, "Calvinism and 'The Judicial Law of Moses,'" *The Journal of Christian Reconstruction*, 5, no. 2 (Winter 1978–1979): 17–38.

85. Sinclair B. Ferguson, "An Assembly of Theonomists? The Teaching of the Westminster Divines on the Law of God," in *Theonomy: A Reformed Critique*, ed. William S. Barker and W. Robert Godfrey (Grand Rapids: Zondervan, 1990), 326–34.

"disasters." He gave only qualified approval to the notion of "just war," saying, "But, say they, the wise man will wage just wars. As if he would not all the rather lament the necessity of just wars, if he remembers that he is a man; for if they were not just he would not wage them, and would therefore be delivered from all wars. For it is the wrongdoing of the opposing party which compels the wise man to wage just wars."[86] Medieval theologian Thomas Aquinas (1225–1274), leaning heavily on Augustine, systematized the requirements for a war to be just in its reasons and manner of prosecution.[87]

Roland Bainton (1894–1984) said there are three basic approaches to war: "pacifism, the just war, and the crusade."[88] In Bainton's view, the crusade or holy war invoked God's approval so that no standards of justice or mercy applied.[89] Bainton accused the Puritans of setting aside the just war doctrine and promoting a religious crusade or holy war.[90] However, James Turner Johnson writes, "Bainton does not take into account that those whom he terms 'crusaders' understood themselves to be squarely within the just war tradition, and in particular the Puritans derived their thought on war directly from the classic Christian doctrine." Johnson also observes, "To single out the Puritans as English 'crusaders' is to overlook all the other classes of Englishmen who at about the same time were clamoring for religious war on the basis of their own various preferences in religion,"[91] not to mention the many bloody and protracted wars against Protestant communities incited by the papacy.

---

86. Augustine, *City of God*, 19.7, trans. Marcus Dods, in *Nicene and Post-Nicene Fathers, Series 1*, ed. Philip Schaff (Buffalo: The Christian Literature Co., 1887), 2:405.

87. Thomas Aquinas, *Summa Theologica*, trans. Fathers of the English Dominican Province (London: R. & T. Washbourne, 1917), Second Part of the Second Part, Q. 40.

88. Roland H. Bainton, *Christian Attitudes toward War and Peace: A Historical Survey and Critical Re-evaluation* (New York: Abingdon, 1960), 14. Bainton was a renowned historian of the Reformation who had pacifist beliefs and close personal connections to the Quakers.

89. Bainton, *Christian Attitudes toward War and Peace*, 49. Bainton viewed the biblical histories of Israel's conquest in Canaan as the product of later writers ("Deuteronomists"), not Moses (47).

90. Bainton, *Christian Attitudes toward War and Peace*, 147–51. His thesis is generally followed by Timothy George, "War and Peace in the Puritan Tradition," *Church History* 53, no. 4 (December 1984): 492–503.

91. James Turner Johnson, *Ideology, Reason, and the Limitation of War: Religious and Secular Concepts, 1200–1740* (Princeton, N.J.: Princeton University Press, 1975), 10.

An example of the just war theory outlined by Augustine and Thomas Aquinas, and mediated through Renaissance philosophy, is described by William Ames.[92] Ames said that war in itself is evil, and only a "cruel man" goes to war "simply desiring it and delighting in it." However, waging war may be lawful and warranted in certain circumstances.[93] Following the classic doctrine, Ames said that just war requires a "just cause," and after other solutions have failed, a "just authority" to initiate and lead the war, a "right intention" for justice and peace, and a "just manner of waging" war in accordance with God's law.[94] A just war aims to attack only the guilty party, seeking to harm "neither children nor ordinarily women, nor indeed quiet [not hostile] men," not plundering, pillaging, or raping.[95] The aim of just war is not to destroy, but to establish justice and peace.

Thomas Adams (1583–1652) approached the doctrine of just war with sober realism. He said, "War is that miserable desolation that finds a land before it like Eden, and leaves it behind like Sodom and Gomorrah, a desolate and forsaken wilderness."[96] He exclaimed, "Happy are we that cannot judge the terrors of war but by report and hearsay!"[97] Drawing upon Augustine, Adams said, "In war seek peace.... Let necessity put war into the hands, religion keep peace in the heart."[98] He encouraged soldiers by saying "that war at sometimes is just and necessary; indeed, just when it is necessary" because the people are in danger of losing their peace, safety, or most of all, the gospel of Jesus Christ by the invasion of foreign persecutors.[99] However, war should be limited by compassion, he said, and

---

92. Johnson detects in Ames the influence of Francisco de Vitoria or Franciscus de Victoria (d. 1546), a Spanish Catholic philosopher who wrote *De jure belli*, though noting that Ames went beyond Vitoria in prohibiting the plunder of noncombatants. Johnson, *Ideology, Reason, and the Limitation of War*, 171–74, 200–202.

93. Ames, *Conscience with the Power and Cases Thereof*, 5.33.2–9 (184–85).

94. Ames, *Conscience with the Power and Cases Thereof*, 5.33.11–14 (186).

95. Ames, *Conscience with the Power and Cases Thereof*, 5.33.30–36 (190–91).

96. Thomas Adams, *The Soldier's Honour*, in *The Works of Thomas Adams* (1861–1866; repr., Eureka, Cal.: Tanski, 1998), 1:37.

97. Adams, *The Soldier's Honour*, in *Works*, 1:40.

98. Adams, *The Soldier's Honour*, in *Works*, 1:38.

99. Adams, *The Soldier's Honour*, in *Works*, 1:41–43.

the Christian soldier must not strike down those who surrender, nor take advantage of the unfortunate.[100]

Gouge placed restrictions on warfare similar to those of Ames to minimize excessive bloodshed against enemies and violence against women, children, and the elderly. He also called men of war to great watchfulness over themselves to avoid "pride, wrath, revenge, cruelty, and many other corruptions" to which men are prone when gathered in an army.[101] Gouge acknowledged that in "extraordinary cases" God gave special instructions to His people to utterly destroy a people, such as the Canaanites and the Amalekites, but Gouge said those are not examples for us to imitate,[102] for we do not have the warrant of God's direct revelation commanding us to do so.[103] All our wars today should be just wars.

---

100. Adams, *The Soldier's Honour*, in *Works*, 1:43. Adams was counted by George among the Puritans advocating holy war. George, "War and Peace in the Puritan Tradition," 495. It is true that Adams echoed the Bible's language of God as a warrior, saw the martial victories of Christians as providential, and invoked Deut. 13 to justify fighting for the gospel. However, he explained "God's battles" not as offensive wars to impose religion on other nations, but as defensive wars when "there is hazard to lose the peace of the people, the safety of the country, [and] the glory of all, the gospel of our Saviour Christ." At the time (1617), Protestant England was still threatened by Roman Catholic Spain, with whom they had fought a series of battles (1586–1604). Furthermore, he limited a soldier's use of violence to the battlefield and forbade him to "strike the yielding" or "prey upon" the weak (1:43).

101. William Gouge, *God's Three Arrowes: Plague, Famine, Sword* (London: by George Miller for Edward Brewster, 1631), 3.60, 91 (293, 295, 351).

102. Gouge, *God's Three Arrowes*, 3.60 (295–96). In this regard, Ames and Gouge stood in stark contrast to Henry Bullinger (1504–1575), who argued from the Old Testament that God requires magistrates to "kill without pity or mercy" incorrigible enemies or rebels. *The Decades of Henry Bullinger: The First and Second Decades*, trans. H. I., ed. Thomas Harding (Cambridge: Cambridge University Press, 1849), 376 (Dec. 2, Serm. 9).

103. Gouge, *God's Three Arrowes*, 3.18 (214–15). Some of Gouge's statements have provoked the accusation by Johnson, Cahill, and Larson that Gouge promoted holy war against Roman Catholics akin to ancient Israel's slaughter of entire peoples. Gouge did commend religious wars "against Anti-Christ" for the "maintenance of truth, and purity of religion" (3.18 [215]). Gouge also made the ominous statement that "Papists to Protestants are as Amalekites to Israelites" (3.3 [188]), which some have taken as a justification for wholesale slaughter. However, in its context, Gouge's statement comparing "Papists" to "Amalekites" referred to Roman Catholic hatred against Protestants, and said nothing of Protestant war against Romanists, which is addressed in a later portion of his book. When he did address just war, Gouge observed that Israel's massacres of the Canaanites were warranted by God's express command, and commented, "If any will make those wars a pattern to root

*Fifth: Civil Establishment of True Religion*

The Puritans believed that a civil magistrate should promote true religion and punish false religion.[104] Ames said, "The chief care of the magistrate ought to be, that he promote true religion, and repress impiety," though he must not trespass into the distinct calling of the church's ministers, for he is a political ruler, not an ecclesiastical ruler.[105] Ames wrote, "Magistracy is an ordinance of God the Creator and belongs to all kinds of men, but the ecclesiastical ministry is a gift and ordinance of Christ the Mediator and properly and commonly belongs only to those who are of the church of Christ."[106] Thus, Ames believed that if heretics (false teachers who contradict principal doctrines) are "publicly hurtful," then the magistrate should use force to restrain them, and even kill them if they are openly blasphemous and obstinate.[107]

The Puritans and Scottish Presbyterians applied this principle in a variety of ways. Samuel Rutherford utterly rejected religious

---

out kingdoms and nations as Moses and Joshua did, let them show the like warrant" (3.18 [214–15]). Lacking such direct revelation, we have no right to conduct wars of extermination today. Therefore, it is not accurate to portray Gouge as "an extreme among Puritan writers," as Johnson did (cf. George). Rather, as Juster observed, Gouge stood at some distance from extreme British calls to holy war. Extreme positions are reportedly found in Alexander Leighton (c. 1570–1649) and Thomas Barnes. See Johnson, *Ideology, Reason, and the Limitation of War*, 120–24; Lisa Sowle Cahill, *Love Your Enemies: Discipleship, Pacifism, and Just War Theory* (Minneapolis: Fortress Press, 1994), 145; Larson, *Calvin's Doctrine of the State*, 41–42n30; George, "War and Peace in the Puritan Tradition," 495; Susan Juster, *Sacred Violence in Early America* (Philadelphia: University of Pennsylvania Press, 2016), 88–89; Alexander Leighton, *Speculum Belli Sacri, or, The Looking-glasse of the Holy Warre* (1624); Thomas Barnes, *Vox Belli, or, An Alarum to Warre* (London: by H. L. for Nathanael Newbery, 1626).

104. For Puritan views of religious toleration and liberty in the mid-seventeenth century, see George Yule, *Puritans in Politics: The Religious Legislation of the Long Parliament, 1640–1647*, The Courtenay Library of Reformation Classics 13 (Appleford, England: Sutton Courtenay Press, 1981), 208–234, 371–402; Blair Worden, *God's Instruments: Political Conduct in the England of Oliver Cromwell* (Oxford: Oxford University Press, 2012), 63–90, 316–54.

105. Ames, *Conscience with the Power and Cases Thereof*, 5.15.8 (165). See David W. Hall, *Savior or Servant? Putting Government in Its Place* (Oak Ridge, Tenn.: The Kuyper Institute, 1996), 241–42.

106. Ames, *The Marrow of Theology*, 2.17.48 (311).

107. Ames, *Conscience with the Power and Cases Thereof*, 4.4.12–15 (12). For example, the Pelagian denial of original sin would be a heresy in his view. Ames did not regard most Anabaptists, Arminians, or Lutherans to be heretics, or even many who were "Papists" through ignorance or fear (4.4.6–11 [10–12]).

liberty. He argued for the civil enforcement of all matters revealed by God, though not inner belief but only outward expressions of doctrine and worship as defined by a legally established Presbyterianism.[108] The English Congregationalists called for established national religion and church and a limited civil tolerance of orthodox Christianity, which happened to some extent under Cromwell's Protectorate through the influence of theologians like John Owen.[109] Similarly, but with wider inclusiveness, Baxter called for religious tolerance of all who affirmed the Apostles' Creed, the Ten Commandments, and the Lord's Prayer, but not "unlimited liberty," for, he said, civil magistrates should punish those who preach heresy or who publicly revile established religion.[110] Others who shared some of the beliefs of Puritanism but called for an even broader religious liberty included John Goodwin (1594–1665),[111] John Milton (1608–1674),[112] and Roger Williams (c. 1603–1683).[113]

---

108. Thus throughout Rutherford, *A Free Disputation against Pretended Liberty of Conscience.* See Daniel Saxton, "'The Ablest Defence of Persecution During the Seventeenth Century': A Historical Assessment of Samuel Rutherford's *A Free Disputation against Pretended Liberty of Conscience*" (MA thesis, Westminster Seminary California, 2013), 52–55; Crawford Gribben, "Samuel Rutherford and Liberty of Conscience," in *Samuel Rutherford*, ed. Vogan, 265–91.

109. John Owen, *Of Toleration*, in *Works*, 8:163–206; James Maclear, "The Birth of the Free Church Tradition," *Church History* 26, no. 2 (June 1957): 99–131; Samuel Pearson, Jr., "Reluctant Radicals: The Independents at the Westminster Assembly," *Journal of Church and State* 11, no. 3 (Autumn 1969): 473–86; Carolyn Polizzotto, "Liberty of Conscience and the Whitehall Debates of 1648–9," *Journal of Ecclesiastical History* 26, no. 1 (January 1975): 69–82; W. K. Jordan, *The Development of Religious Toleration in England, Volume 3, From the Convention of the Long Parliament to the Restoration, 1640–1660* (Gloucester, Mass.: Peter Smith, 1965); John Coffey, *Persecution and Toleration in Protestant England, 1558–1689* (London: Routledge, 2000).

110. Baxter, *A Christian Directory*, 4.11.38–39 (800).

111. Goodwin was an Arminian Congregationalist theologian. See John Coffey, *John Goodwin and the Puritan Revolution: Religion and Intellectual Change in Seventeenth-Century England* (Woodbridge, Eng.: Boydell, 2008).

112. Milton wrote several tracts on liberty, including his influential defense of freedom of speech, *Areopagitica* (London, 1644). See Sharon Achinstein and Elizabeth Sauer, eds, *Milton and Toleration* (Oxford: Oxford University Press, 2007); Witte, *The Reformation of Rights*, 219–75.

113. Williams, author of *The Bloudy Tenent of Persecution* (London, 1644), was trained in the Church of England and might be considered a Puritan in his early years, but later became a Separatist, then a Baptist, and ultimately renounced all churches though continuing to confess faith in Christ. For the influence of Congregationalists like John Owen and especially the more radical Williams upon John

*Sixth: Human Rights and Accountability of Rulers*

Contrary to popular belief, the idea of basic human rights and liberties did not originate in the Enlightenment, but was articulated "in classical Rome and in medieval Catholic Europe," and reasserted in the Reformation, as John Witte observes.[114] Calvin wrote of "the common rights of mankind" and "natural rights," including property rights, marital rights, the rights of parents, and the rights of the poor and oppressed.[115] He linked a person's "right to liberty," and called its denial "tyranny."[116]

The idea that all men have certain rights as human beings created in God's image is linked with the belief that civil rulers have only limited authority over men. Many Puritans, in continuity with early English Reformer and Marian exile John Ponet (c. 1514–1556), rejected the "divine right of kings" theory which made the king accountable to God alone, and asserted that the king was accountable to his people when he violated God's laws.[117] The deep historical roots of a people's rights and liberties under the king were presaged in the English Magna Carta (1215) and asserted in the British Petition of Right (1628), which prohibited taxation without representation in Parliament, imprisonment or fines without due process of law (as often happens under conditions of martial law), and quartering troops in private homes.[118]

The Puritans articulated the biblical basis of these political ideas. Rutherford argued from Old Testament history that "there is an oath betwixt the king and his people," an express covenant

---

Locke's view of religious toleration, see Winthrop S. Hudson, "John Locke: Heir of Puritan Political Theorists," in *Calvinism and the Political Order*, 108–129.

114. John Witte, Jr., *The Reformation of Rights: Law, Religion, and Human Rights in Early Modern Calvinism* (Cambridge: Cambridge University Press, 2007), 23.

115. Witte, *The Reformation of Rights*, 58–59. For example, see Calvin, *Commentaries*, on Gen. 1:28; 4:13; 16:1; 21:14–16, 20; Isa. 58:7; 1 Cor. 7:11.

116. Calvin, *Commentaries*, on Gen. 9:3.

117. John Ponet, *A Shorte Treatise of Politike Power* (1556; repr. 1639, 1642). John Adams (1735–1826), second president of the United States, stated that Ponet's book "contains all the essential principles of liberty" later expounded by John Locke. John Adams, *A Defence of the Constitutions of the Government of the United States of America, Against the Attack of M. Turgot*, new ed. (London: John Stockdale, 1794), 3:210.

118. William Dunn, *A History of Political Theories* (New York: Macmillan, 1905), 2:222. On early modern English views of human rights, see Quentin Skinner, *Liberty before Liberalism* (Cambridge: Cambridge University Press, 1998).

in the presence of God, that lays upon both parties "mutual civil obligation."[119] David McKay writes, "Rutherford emphasizes that all men are born equally free and that none naturally has authority over others. Thus he demolishes at a stroke the claim of any to be born to rule."[120] Rutherford said civil authority is from God (Rom. 13:1), and kings and magistrates are "God's deputies and lieutenants upon earth" (Ps. 82:1, 6, 7; Ex. 22:8; 4:16), but the particular form of government and persons in that government are appointed by the people (1 Chron. 12:38), whether authority resides in a supreme king (monarchy), a group of leaders (aristocracy), or the citizens (democracy).[121] Thus civil authority is not based on a *social contract* in which people surrender their natural liberties and rights to gain the protection of government,[122] nor is any particular ruler or government established by *divine right*, but civil authority is established by God and implemented by the covenantal consent of the people. In reality, Rutherford argued, all governments that avoid the extremes of anarchy and tyranny are a mixture of democracy, aristocracy, and monarchy, for government must seek the public good, rule by a multitude of counselors, and be united under one leader.[123] The political

---

119. Rutherford, *Lex, Rex*, Q. 14 (54). He cited 2 Sam. 5:3; 1 Chron. 11:3; 2 Chron. 23:2–3; 2 Kings 11:17; Eccl. 8:2. It is interesting to note that in the United States, any officer of the government from the President down swears an oath to uphold the Constitution, commonly concluded with the words, "So help me God."

120. McKay, "Samuel Rutherford on Civil Government," in *Samuel Rutherford*, 254.

121. Rutherford, *Lex, Rex*, Q. 1, 3, 4 (1, 4, 6). Compare Ames: "The superiority of power, or government itself is simply and absolutely commanded by God, and in that respect is called the ordinance of God [Rom. 13:1–2]; but this or that special manner of power or government is not determined by God, but by men; and is therefore called 'an ordinance of man.'" William Ames, *An Analyticall Exposition of Both the Epistles of the Apostle Peter* (London: by E. G. for John Rothwell, 1641), 58 (on 1 Peter 2:13).

122. Hall, *Savior or Servant*, 243. This is the position of Thomas Hobbes, Locke, and Jean-Jacques Rousseau.

123. Rutherford, *Lex, Rex*, Q. 24 (116). He said, "A limited and mixed monarchy, such as is in Scotland and England, seems to be the best government, when parliaments, with the good, have the good of all three. This government hath glory, order, unity, from a monarch; from the government of the most and wisest, it hath safety of counsel, stability, strength; from the influence of the commons, it hath liberty, privileges, promptitude of obedience." *Lex, Rex*, Q. 38 (192). See Calvin, *Institutes*, 4.20.8, though Calvin favored a mixture of aristocracy and democracy. The idea of a "mixed constitution" that balances elements of different forms of governments for the sake of justice and stability goes back to ancient Greek philosophy, Roman

covenant binds the king to "rule according to God's law."[124] Even if a government was not inaugurated with a formal covenant, Rutherford asserted that "the law of nature" makes the right to exercise authority conditional upon "those things which are just and right according to the law of God."[125] Many of the principles of limited government were incorporated into the Massachusetts Body of Liberties (1641) and the English Bill of Rights (1689), which were foundational documents for the United States Constitution (ratified 1789).

The most enduring legacy of the Puritans on governance is included in Chapter 20 of the Westminster Confession of Faith, "Of Christian Liberty, and Liberty of Conscience." The Westminster divines articulated a very careful and thorough definition of Christian liberty, but went on to declare, "God alone is Lord of the conscience, and hath left it free from the doctrines and commandments of men which are in anything contrary to His Word; or beside it, in matters of faith or worship" (20.2). In so doing, they laid the foundation for the rights and freedoms of the American people, not to mention many other nations, in regard to personal freedom of religion and the rights of conscience.

### Seventh: Political Resistance to Evil

Reformed theologians from the mid-sixteenth century onward taught that if civil power is abused, lesser magistrates may lead a lawful resistance against it.[126] If the civil magistrate becomes a tyrant, Rutherford said, the people have the right to use military force in

---

republicanism, and their revival in the Renaissance. The US Constitution reflects this principle in its representative democracy overseen by the presidency.

124. Rutherford, *Lex, Rex*, Q. 14 (57).

125. Rutherford, *Lex, Rex*, Q. 14 (59).

126. Calvin, *Institutes*, 4.20.31–32; *Commentaries* (repr., Grand Rapids: Baker, 2003), on Dan. 6:22. On the development of this doctrine from its seed in early Lutheranism to its full appropriation and application by Reformed theologians, see Quentin Skinner, *The Foundations of Modern Political Thought, Volume 2, The Age of Reformation* (Cambridge: Cambridge University Press, 1978), 189–348; Esther Hildebrandt, "The Magdeburg Bekenntnis as a Possible Link Between German and English Resistance Theories in the Sixteenth Centuries," *Archiv für Reformationsgeschichte* 71 (1980): 227–53; David H. Wollman, "The Biblical Justification for Resistance to Authority in Ponet's and Goodman's Polemics," *Sixteenth Century Journal* 13, no. 4 (1982): 29–41; Richard C. Gamble, "The Christian and the Tyrant: Beza and Knox on Political Resistance Theory," *Westminster Theological Journal* 46 (1984): 125–39; Witte, "Law, Authority, and Liberty," in *Calvin and Culture*, 26–30.

self-defense, just as a man may use violence against a robber who breaks into his home at night (cf. Ex. 22:2). Thus in fleeing from King Saul, David was warranted in taking Goliath's sword, and gathering six hundred men to defend himself.[127] However, warfare must be the last resort, only used if supplication and appeal to the authority fails and flight to safety is impractical (as in the case of a whole community).[128]

Resisting a civil authority does not justify anarchy or lawlessness, Rutherford said, but must be done in a lawful manner under the leadership of other civil authorities, just as Calvin had taught,[129] for even lesser officials appointed by the king are servants of the Lord accountable to God, not just the deputies of the king (2 Chron. 19:5–6).[130] All civil officials, high or low, are appointed by God to do good to the people and to punish evil-doers (Rom. 13:1–3), and therefore no one official has absolute power over the other officials so that he cannot be resisted by them.[131]

Rutherford said, "Those who make the king…have the power to unmake him."[132] If a civil magistrate abuses his power "to the destruction of laws, religion, and subjects," then we are under no obligation to submit to him.[133] According to Rutherford, the command to submit to civil powers in Romans 13 speaks of the rightful office of a magistrate considered abstractly as God's ordinance, and does not apply to the exercise of "abused and tyrannical power."[134] In this he agreed with the distinction made by Scottish Reformer John Knox (c. 1514–1572), who wrote, "All authority which God hath established is good and perfect, and is to be obeyed…. But do ye not understand that there is a great difference betwixt the authority

---

127. Rutherford, *Lex, Rex*, Q. 31, 32 (159–60, 166–72). He cited other examples of resistance against civil authority in 1 Sam. 14:44–45; 23:8–13; 2 Sam. 20:18–20; 2 Kings 6:32; 2 Chron. 21:10; 26:17.

128. Rutherford, *Lex, Rex*, Q. 31 (160).

129. "Magistrates of the people [are] appointed to restrain the willfulness of kings," and must "withstand, in accordance with their duty, the fierce licentiousness of kings," lest the magistrates "betray the freedom of the people." Calvin, *Institutes*, 4.20.31.

130. Rutherford, *Lex, Rex*, Q. 20 (88).

131. Rutherford, *Lex, Rex*, Q. 20 (91–93).

132. Rutherford, *Lex, Rex*, Q. 31 (98).

133. Rutherford, *Lex, Rex*, Q. 28 (141).

134. Rutherford, *Lex, Rex*, Q. 29 (144–46).

which is God's ordinance and the persons of those which are placed in authority?"[135]

In summary, the Puritans generally advocated a view of politics in which God delegated civil authority to some men through the consent of the people for the benefit of the people. A civil magistrate must use his powers, including the sword, to maintain peace, justice, and the promotion of true religion. Though the Puritans believed people should bear with the faults of their king, they also believed that if the king persistently oppressed the people, they could resist him, even replace him with another ruler, in a manner consistent with the laws of God. In making such assertions, the Puritans were not blazing new trails so much as arguing for political principles already found in the medieval Catholic conciliar movement, Spanish Thomistic philosophy, and the sixteenth-century Reformed tradition.[136]

Of course, the Puritans engaged in politics in their own culture and time, when kings and national churches were wedded to the civil government. We cannot follow them woodenly in their political theories, policies, and practices. In the United States today, most Christians have a view of religious liberty that very few Puritans shared. Christians today debate the proper application of Mosaic judicial laws to the modern state. However, even in politics the Puritans operated out of a God-centered worldview, arguing that human sovereignty derives from divine sovereignty, which both legitimizes civil government and limits its authority. We also note that the Puritan worldview of *fatherly* sovereignty required that political leaders use their authority with fatherly benevolence, for if they act as tyrants they misrepresent the Lord God.

## Conclusion: The God-Centered Puritan Worldview

The Puritans built a worldview based upon the Holy Scriptures to encompass every facet of human life. Just as the sun dominates the sky with its brilliant light, so the Puritan worldview was illuminated by God's benevolent sovereignty over all things in Jesus Christ. The Puritans sought to walk in the light of the Lord in every cultural

---

135. John Knox, *Letters to the Regent and Nobility*, in *Knox: On Rebellion*, ed. Roger A. Mason, Cambridge Texts in the History of Political Thought (Cambridge: Cambridge University Press, 1994), 154.

136. Coffey, *Politics*, 158.

endeavor and human relationship. They did not limit their devotion to God to private piety, but sought to be salt and light in this world, resisting evil and bringing the light of Christ to the nations. Though they often failed to accomplish their aims, their worldview is still full of truth, beauty, and glory.

Since the time of the Puritans, our understanding of God's Word has altered as our cultural situation has changed. Some applications of the Puritan worldview are outdated and obsolete. However, God remains the same, His word never changes, and the human race continues to suffer from its bondage to sin and misery which only Jesus Christ and His gospel can remedy.

I challenge you to stand on the shoulders of the Puritans. Do not simply copy them but learn from them and let them drive you deeper into God's Word. I challenge you to refuse to leave the wisdom of God's Word at home when you go to school, to work, and into the public square. Do not walk in the counsel of the ungodly, or stand in the way of sinners, or sit in the seat of scorners. Instead, allow God's Word to illuminate your whole mind and motivate your whole life. Do not be a hearer of the Word only, but also a doer of the Word.

In particular, I challenge you to formulate a biblical view of economics and politics. Read the news with your Bible open. Read the Puritans and other Reformed Christians on these matters. Discuss contemporary issues with wise Christians. Use the vocation to which God has called you to do as much good as you can. And may God use the writings of the Reformers and Puritans to raise up a generation that is truly salt and light to the world around them. And remember, as the Puritans often reminded us: we are but pilgrims and strangers here in this world, seeking a better country as citizens of Zion, the beautiful city of God.

# FORMATIVE TRUTHS FOR
# THE CHRISTIAN'S LIFE

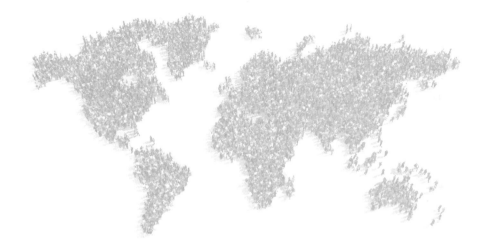

# CHAPTER 4

# The Christian Worldview
# for Daily Life
## Colossians 3:1–17

*Derek W. H. Thomas*

When I think of New Testament summaries that encapsulate the nature or worldview of the Christian life, there are several Scripture passages that come to mind. I think especially of Romans 6. And more and more, I think of that passage as key and fundamental to our understanding of the shape and the contours of the Christian life: the believer is buried with Christ and risen with Christ. That is the new identity of the one who trusts in Jesus Christ. We are no longer who we once were.

Another key that captures the essence of the Christian life is Galatians 2:20: "I am crucified with Christ: nevertheless I live; yet not I, but Christ liveth in me: and the life which I now live in the flesh I live by the faith of the Son of God, who loved me, and gave himself for me." Here, too, Paul is giving expression to how a Christian should think about his or her identity. It is no longer the old Adamic self that lives but a new identity, one who lives in union and communion with Christ.

I think also of the passage we will explore here, Colossians 3:1–17. Along with Romans 6 and Galatians 2:20, this passage also provides us with a mountain range from which we may view the broad contours of the Christian life. And in order to understand what it is saying, we need something of the context in which it was written. In summary, the Colossians had lost sight of two things: *who Christ is* and *who they were*. Both losses are common among Christians, and both losses are catastrophic.

What seems to have happened, and it is what often happens in the Christian life, is that having initially been delivered from the life of sinful habits, and having been delivered from it by the power of the gospel, they then discover that the road to heaven is not a bed of roses. Difficulties and tensions remain. Life continues to demonstrate temptations within and opposition without. And, moreover, those sins from which they were initially delivered by the power of the gospel return because those sins are deeply woven into their hearts and into their lifestyle. The initial deliverance is temporary and shallow. The temptation to return to "old habits" was (and is) all too powerful. And therefore a question arises: how can we be *totally* delivered from sin?

And present at Colossae was a ready answer. The "solution" took a certain form: "What you need is an experience of *fullness* and you will be delivered." In fact, this word "fullness" seems to have been something of a buzzword in Colossae. "The gospel and what you have experienced is all very well, but you need something in addition to that so that you can experience real *fullness*." And Paul responds without equivocation: "You don't need to *acquire* fullness because you *already have it* in union and communion with the risen and reigning Jesus Christ." Being a Christian involves realizing and acknowledging who *Jesus is* and who *you are* in union with Jesus Christ. That is the key and the secret to powerful, victorious Christian living.

With that in mind, let us explore four lines of thought based on Colossians 3 on living out the Christian worldview in our daily lives.

### The Shape of Apostolic Teaching

There is an apostolic *shape* to the Christian worldview and the entirety of the Christian life. It is the silhouette that issues from the gospel. The gospel saves us from sin and its consequences and delivers us into the arms of the Lord Jesus. But it does so, as long as we remain in this world, in stages. The glory that is promised in the gospel is a new existence in heaven and ultimately in the new heaven and new earth. But so long as we remain in *this* world, there is a constant and unrelenting opposition. The Christian life is lived in the tension between the now and the not yet. As the apostle John describes it, "Now are we the sons of God, and it doth not yet appear what we shall be" (1 John 3:2). We are not what we were; but neither are we what we shall be. The first thing to realize about the shape of the Christian life in this world is that it is always an experience of tension.

First of all, this tension is played out on the grand scale of redemptive history. In the Old Testament there is a tension between prophecy and fulfillment. There is an anticipation of the coming of the fulfillment of a promise, of a seed that will crush the head of Satan, a prophet that will arise and reveal the things of God, a Messiah who will come and relieve us of the burden of our sin. And in the birth, life, death, and resurrection of Jesus Christ, this tension is relieved.

Secondly, a new tension develops within the New Testament era. The "last days" dawn with the coming of the Holy Spirit (cf. Acts 2:17; Heb. 1:2; 2 Pet. 3:3). In one specific sense, Christianity is a "new-age" religion. We are those upon whom the end of the ages has dawned (1 Cor. 10:11). We have tasted of the goodness of the Word of God, the powers of the Word of God, and the powers of the age to come (Heb. 6:1–4).

And while we are in this world, we simultaneously belong to two worlds: this one and the one to come. The Colossian Christians live in this world, in a place called *Colossae*: "Paul, an apostle of Jesus Christ by the will of God, and Timotheus our brother, to the saints and faithful brethren in Christ which are at Colosse" (Col. 1:1, 2). Where are these brothers and sisters of Paul? They are in a place called Colossae. They are in a city. They are in this world. They have jobs and homes; they walk the streets; they live their lives; they have marriages, families, children, and concerns. They are part of this world. And like them, we too have an identity that roots us in this world.

But in addition, Christians have another identity. We are "in Christ." We are in union and communion with Christ who has ascended, who is sitting at the right hand of God, who occupies the throne of the universe. We are in this world, but we are also in union and communion with Christ. We are part of the here and now, but we are also part of the not yet. We are here but we are also in Christ and in communion with Him who sits enthroned in the heavens. It is part of the fundamental shape of the gospel that we have these two realities, two spiritual zip codes. It is how Paul begins this epistle to the Colossians. So the Christian life is fundamentally lived in the tension between what we are now and what we shall be because of our union and communion with Christ, a union that can never be severed. It is a fundamental aspect of the Christian worldview and the Christian life.

Thirdly, the Christian life is lived in the tension of what is true now and what needs to be true—the tension between the indicatives and the imperatives. There were people in Colossae coming and saying, "You need to have this fullness." In the twentieth century it might have come in this form: "You need the baptism of the Spirit." According to this view, being a Christian is a substandard life. And in order to experience fullness one needs something extra, such as a baptism of the Spirit. It is sometimes put this way: A Christian needs to get out of the struggle of Romans 7 into the certainty and assurance of Romans 8 and the victorious Christian life that it portrays. This is, of course, fundamentally mistaken since one of the imperatives insisted upon in Romans 8 is the mortification of ongoing sin (Rom. 8:13). There is tension and struggle in Romans 8 too!

In Colossians, Paul is drawing attention to the fact that a Christian already has fullness, and that fullness is in union and communion with Christ. In Colossians 2:9 we read, "For in him dwelleth all the fulness of the Godhead bodily." Verse 10 continues: "And ye are complete in him." If you are in Christ you are in union with the one who is God and you lack nothing. You have all the resources to live the Christian life in union and communion with the fullness of God that dwells in Jesus Christ, "which is the head of all principality and power: in whom also ye are circumcised with the circumcision made without hands, in putting off the body of the sins of the flesh by the circumcision of Christ: buried with him in baptism, wherein also ye are risen with him through the faith of the operation of God, who hath raised him from the dead" (Col 2:10–12).

Paul engages, then, in logical and consequential thinking. Technically he employs the grammatical formula of *protasis* and *apodosis*—clauses which begin with an "if" and conclude with a "then." "If ye then be risen with Christ" (Col. 3:1). If this is true, then that is true. These things are true, therefore these things are true. He is thinking logically. Because you are in Christ, and Christ is the fullness of God, then certain things follow; there are certain consequences. If these indicatives are true, then here are the imperatives—"seek those things which are above."

This is not a "pull yourself up by your bootstraps" philosophy or theology. Paul is making a very fundamental point here. Because you are in union and communion with Christ, certain imperatives are in order. The imperative follows the indicative. What we are being asked to do (and we *are* being asked to do something), is not a form of legalism. We must be very clear about that. Discussions about law and gospel often confuse the place of an imperative in the Christian life. It is fundamental here in Colossians 3 that there is a relationship between what is indicative—what is true *of* or *about* us—and what this truth demands of us by way of consequence.

Of course, these imperatives are not worked out entirely by us as though Jesus does everything in the gospel to save you and then leaves you entirely to yourself to work out the rest of your life. God works in us by the Holy Spirit to accomplish the very imperatives he demands of us. Progressive sanctification is thus synergistic and cooperative. "Work out your own salvation with fear and trembling. For it is God which worketh in you both to will and to do of his good pleasure" (Phil. 2:12–13). This is a fundamental, apostolic shape of the Christian worldview of daily living.

### The Identity that Every Christian Believer Receives

Every Christian needs to be reminded of who they are. A form of spiritual amnesia takes place while we sleep at night and it is vital that we begin each new day reminding ourselves of who we are. Look next at verse 9: "Lie not one to another, seeing that ye have put off the old man with his deeds." There is an imperative here: don't lie. Why? Because of *who you are* and because of fundamental changes that have taken place in your life. You are no longer a part of the "old" man. You have put off the old man with his deeds, "and have put on the new man, which is renewed in knowledge after the image of him that created him" (v. 10). You are no longer in Adam; instead, you are in Christ. You have taken off your old self and have put on the new self. Look at how he puts it in Colossians 2:12: "Buried with him in baptism, wherein also ye are risen with him through the faith of the operation of God, who hath raised him from the dead." Just as he does in Romans 6, he uses the metaphor of changing our clothing—putting off and putting on. Note what he is saying: you have died to the old order of things. He is talking to believers in Colossae, those who have put their faith in the Lord Jesus, and have found themselves in union and communion with Christ.

Additionally, look at Colossians 2:20: "Wherefore if ye be dead with Christ." You are dead to what you once were. You are no longer in Adam. Rather, you are a new creation in Christ. You have been buried, you have been pronounced dead and put in a tomb. And you have come to new life. As he puts it in 3:3, "Ye are dead, and your life is hid with Christ in God." That is who you are. That is your identity. You are no longer what you once were. You can't blame your Adamic self for sins that you commit as a Christian.

Realize your identity. Who are you? It is something we ought to ask ourselves every morning when we awake. When we look at ourselves in the mirror, we ought to say, "Who is that? Who am I looking at? I am looking at a person in Christ." I am no longer looking at the old self, the Adamic self. I am someone who is now in union and communion with Christ and indwelt by the Holy Spirit of God. My life is hidden with Christ in God. Tell yourself that every morning. We are caught up with Christ so that when He appears we shall appear with Him in glory.

Who are you? If you are a Christian, then you can reply, "I am a person in Christ. My life is hidden with Christ in God, and I shall appear with Him in glory." It provides the motivation for my Christian life.

John Owen is extraordinarily helpful here. In Volume 7 of his collected writings, in the section *The Grace and Duty Of Being Spiritually Minded*[1], he suggested the following test: What do you think about when you're not thinking about anything in particular?[2] What is the default setting of your mind, of your heart, of your affections, of your will? I think the answer to those questions says a lot about us. Is it my inclination that I want to be like Jesus? Do I want to be rid of this sinful life, and these sinful habits? Do I want to destroy them and to kill them? Do I want them out of my life? Do I want to live the victorious Christian life? How do I do that? Well, first realize who you are.

In the second part of *Pilgrim's Progress*, the story of *Christiana* and the four boys, John Bunyan describes the occasion when they are passing through the house of the Interpreter and they see a man, a Christian, whose head is looking at the muck on the floor before him, but above him he doesn't see that there's a beautiful crown. Perhaps this is a description of you! You need to look up and realize who you are and realize what it is that Christ has done for you in regeneration, in justification by faith, in adoption, in bringing you into fellowship

---

1. John Owen, *The Works of John Owen* (London: The Banner of Truth, 1965).
2. John Owen, *Works*, 7:274–81.

with Himself. Jesus said, "Where your treasure is, there will your heart be also" (Matt. 6:21). Where is your treasure?

We must recognize who we are in Christ, and we must have the motivation and discipline to distance ourselves from the patterns of this world, looking to the next. These are some of the contours that Paul implies here as he addresses the Christian worldview as it relates to daily life.

## The Focus on Destroying Remaining Sin

Colossians 3:5–12 emphasizes the need to deal with sin urgently and decisively.

First, Paul makes us face the fact that *sin needs to be dealt with*. "Mortify therefore your members which are upon the earth" (v. 5). We are Christians; we are in union with Christ and indwelt by the Holy Spirit. We are adopted into the household and family of God. Our lives are hidden with Christ in God so that when He appears we shall appear with Him in glory. But the fact is that we are still sinners. That is the dilemma. "For the good that I would I do not: but the evil which I would not, that I do.... O wretched man that I am! Who shall deliver me from the body of this death?" (Rom. 7:19, 24). That is our experience. He makes us face the fact that sin exists, and not just sin in general but identifiable sins with names that need to be dealt with. So first of all, Paul seems to be saying, "Allow yourself to be exposed to the searing eye of God the Holy Spirit and of the Holy Word of God." Look sin in the eye. Name the poisons that are destroying your life.

I was raised on a dairy farm in Wales. We had cows, pigs, chickens, an occasional turkey or two, and every now and then, a goose. My mother had a policy: you don't name anything that was destined for the table. If someone had to take an ax and chop off an animal's head, it was easier to do if no emotional bond existed with the poor creature. It was difficult to enjoy a roast chicken if she had a name. We once had a duck who was originally destined for the Christmas dinner table that we named Charlie. She lived to an old age. She never saw the table. She died in contentment because we gave her a name and my mother couldn't kill her. In the Christian life, the reverse seems to take place. We refuse to name our sins because we want them to survive. Sin is something vague and general: an idea, a notion, a sense, but nothing specific. But sins are very specific. They have names: lust, greed, envy, spite, and so on. We are not serious about dealing with our sins if we cannot name them.

Secondly, Paul reminds us that *when we sin as Christians, we do so in union with Christ*. Look at verse 7: "In the which ye also walked some time, when ye lived in them." There is a certain walk, a certain lifestyle, a certain pattern he refers to here. In the Hebrew it would have the meaning of "instinct," a lifestyle from which we have now been delivered. This lifestyle is incompatible with a person who is in union and communion with Jesus Christ.

J. C. Ryle, in his magnificent book, *Holiness*, wrote in the opening chapter on sin: "He that wishes to attain right views about Christian holiness, must begin by examining the vast and solemn subject of sin."[3] Until you make more of sin you cannot make more of holiness. Think of what we were in the past and think of what we are now in Christ. Paul says in verses 9 and 10 of our passage: "Lie not one to another, seeing that ye have put off the old man with his deeds; and have put on the new man, which is renewed in knowledge after the image of him that created him." He is arguing here in a similar fashion to Romans 5 and 1 Corinthians 15. In both of these chapters, Paul employs the "in Adam" and "in Christ" distinction. Once, we were "in Adam." But now, we are "in Christ." And being in Christ, we are no longer in Adam. That Adamic identity is a thing of the past. Then he writes in verse 11: "Where there is neither Greek nor Jew, circumcision nor uncircumcision, Barbarian, Scythian, bond nor free: but Christ is all, and in all." What is he saying? This is a general principle of the godly Christian life: *Jesus Christ is everything*. Christ in you, the hope of glory. You can't be rid of Christ!

Remember how Paul uses this in an altogether alarming and staggering way in 1 Corinthians 6 when he talks about certain professing believers in Corinth. It is almost incredible and unbelievable that certain believers in Corinth were visiting brothels. And what is Paul's argument here? It is that they can't leave Jesus outside the door! When they sin, they sin in union and communion with Christ! As professing Christians, they cannot blame their sin on their Adamic nature. The Corinthians were in effect taking Christ with them and

---

3. J. C. Ryle, *Holiness: Its Nature, Hindrances, Difficulties, and Roots* (Edinburgh: Banner of Truth Trust, 2014), 1.

uniting Him to a harlot! That is what Paul is saying. That is the implication of it. Realize who you are and that when you sin, you sin in union and communion with Christ. That is the horror of it!

Thirdly, Paul insists that *sin needs to be put to death*. "Mortify therefore your members which are upon the earth" (Col. 3:5). This behavior must be radical. Mortify or put to death all remaining sin. Romans 8:13 advises the same, that we should mortify the deeds of the flesh that we might live. It is a different verb in Greek but the idea is the same—put sin to death.

What is the nature, the philosophy of dealing with sin in the Christian life? Jesus puts it this way: if your right arm offends you, cut it off. If your right eye offends, pluck it out. It is better to go through life maimed with one eye and one arm (Matt. 5:29–30). Some might protest that this sounds legalistic. I think there are some people today who might say so, that it's going too far. For people who think this way, legalism is just a euphemism for saying, "That is just not convenient. I don't want to have to do that right now. I want Jesus but I don't want Jesus at that cost." My dear friends, you don't have a choice. If you have Jesus, if you have the gospel, this is the cost of it! "If any man will come after me, let him deny himself, and take up his cross" (Luke 9:23). What is a cross? It is not a piece of jewelry. When you take Jesus as Lord and Savior, you must be ready to die.

It is easy for some of us to talk about being ready to die for Jesus when martyrdom is a mere theoretical concept. But, for some of our brothers and sisters in certain parts of the world, it is more than a theoretical matter. They are literally having their heads chopped off.

Aspects of this Christian mindset are negative. Sin must be resisted and destroyed. It is the power of negative thinking. The gospel has appeared in order for us to say "no" to sin. It is not complicated. You can make it so philosophically complicated that you don't understand it, but it is not difficult. A believer, someone in union with Christ and indwelt by the Holy Spirit, says, "You've got to put sin to death; you have to say no to it. It is because of these things that the wrath of God is coming upon the world, upon the children of disobedience" (see Colossians 3:6). So what are you doing committing these sins?

The shape and contour of the Christian life involves the desire to put sin to death, to mortify it, to kill it. And it is a lifelong battle, to be sure, with many ups and downs. But the question is this: is the desire there? Do you really want to be rid of this sin, or have you made this sin into a kind of pet that in the confines of your own home and in the secrecy of your own heart you allow out every now and then, and fondle it, and cuddle it, and feed it, and then put it back for another occasion?

There is the power of negative thinking, but there is also the power of positive thinking—to *clothe yourself with Christ*, and with the appropriate graces. There is a negative and a positive. Paul appears to be employing the imagery of the world of "baptism"—particularly in the forefront of advancing missions where the initial converts were adults. There is some evidence that these "adult baptisms" employed a certain ritual whereby they would leave wearing different clothes than the ones they wore upon arrival.[4] Similarly, in progressive sanctification, there is a putting off and a putting on. Clothe yourselves with compassion and kindness, humility and gentleness, and patience (Col. 3:12).

There is a wonderful autobiographical statement by Augustine, a young boy who was converted and made his way to dear Ambrose, an extraordinary preacher. Augustine was greatly blessed by the preaching and ministry of Ambrose. But later he testified it wasn't his preaching that first attracted him to Ambrose; it was his kindness.[5] What an extraordinary thing to say! It was the kindness that Ambrose had shown to Augustine as a young man away from home, in a different country, a different world and environment, that drew him to Ambrose and ultimately to Christ. Ambrose, this great, extraordinary, world-renowned preacher had shown kindness to Augustine.

It's breathtaking to discover how Christians sometimes remember things that people did to them thirty, forty, or fifty years in the past. I remember visiting a certain individual in the past, and every single time I would go there they would bring up this story of an event that occurred so many decades in the past and they had never forgotten it. People say, "I am willing to forgive but I can't forget."

---

4. See the comments by Sinclair Ferguson in *Baptism: Three Views*, edited by David F. Wright, with contributions by Sinclair B. Ferguson, Anthony N. S. Lane, Bruce A. Ware (Downers Grove, Ill.: IVP Academic, 2009).

5. Christopher Hall, *Reading Scripture with the Church Fathers* (Downers Grove, Ill.: InterVarsity Press, 1998), 104.

Well, you *need* to forget! God doesn't bring up your sins every single day and neither should you!

This is the shape of apostolic preaching. This is the identity of Christian believers. This is the imperative that is expected: the mortification and vivification, the putting off and the putting on, the destroying and the bringing to life of the fruits and graces of the Holy Spirit.

### The Means to Live this Christian Life

At the end of this section Paul seems to bring together some principles addressing the means by which the Christian life is to be lived. He says in verse 15, "And let the peace of God rule in your hearts."

At the end of a worship service there is a pronouncement of a benediction. In my tradition the Aaronic benediction is pronounced at the end of a baptism—"The LORD bless thee, and keep thee: the LORD make his face shine upon thee, and be gracious unto thee: the LORD lift up his countenance upon thee, and give thee peace" (Num. 6:24–26). *Shalom*, peace—that is what we invoke at the end of a worship service. Peace, shalom, fullness, completeness in Christ. That is what the gospel has brought about in our lives—completeness and fullness and peace. But that is not what Jesus heard on the cross as our sin-bearer and substitute. It is as if he heard, "The Lord curse you, and shun you, and hide the light of His face from you, and be angry with you, and cast you into hell." That is what He seemed to hear, that we might have peace. Let that peace rule in your heart every moment of every day. "Therefore being justified by faith, we have peace with God through our Lord Jesus Christ" (Rom. 5:1).

What right do I have holding a grudge against another when Jesus has forgiven all my sins and cast them into the sea of His forgetfulness? Notice in our passage the end of verse 15: "Be ye thankful." And at the end of verse 17: "Giving thanks to God and the Father by him." Thankfulness—the amazing imperative, the means by which to live our Christian lives!

An example of this thankfulness that brings me joy in my own life is the tradition of writing thank-you letters. Every week I will have half a dozen thank-you letters from people who took the time to get a pen and hand-write a little thank-you for something. Sometimes it is a trivial thing. But it is an expression of the pattern of their

Christian lives. They are thankful because they have the gospel. We are thankful people because we are forgiven. I am a forgiven person. God has washed my sins away. Therefore, I ought to be thankful every day, even in the midst of trial and difficulty.

Look now at verse 16: "Let the word of Christ dwell in you richly." What is the contour, the shape of the Christian life? It is one that is governed by the authority of the Word of God ministering to us. "All scripture is given by inspiration of God, and is profitable for doctrine, for reproof, for correction, for instruction in righteousness: that the man of God may be perfect, thoroughly furnished unto all good works" (2 Tim. 3:16–17). Let the Word of God dwell in you richly and inform your daily Christian walk.

My dear friend, if you are caught in the grip of the habit of sin, it may be that the Word of God is not dwelling in you richly. You have, in all likelihood, long since abandoned the pattern of reading Scripture for devotional purposes. Establish good, godly Christian habits. Do you love the Word of God? Do you want God to speak to you? Open your Bible and read it because the Bible is God speaking to you. It is His gift to you. And it will make you sing.

Notice how Paul puts it in verse 16: "Let the word of Christ dwell in you richly in all wisdom; teaching and admonishing one another in psalms and hymns and spiritual songs, singing with grace in your hearts to the Lord." The Bible will make you sing. It will make you fall down before Him in worship, praise, and adoration.

And finally, verse 17—"And whatsoever ye do in word or deed, do all in the name of the Lord Jesus." I had an acquaintance with two wonderful sisters, Madge and Anna. When I was first ordained into the ministry, I had the privilege of knowing these two sisters, both of whom were in their eighties. As a young minister, I made it a point to visit them every week on Thursday. They were the sort who were in every meeting no matter what the meeting was about. They just loved the church. On one occasion I was feeling sorry for myself about how difficult the ministry was and how difficult people could be, and I gave vent to my frustrations. One of the sisters looked at me and said, "Young man, see no one in the picture but Jesus." Do you know what I thought when I heard that? I thought, "What a sentimental piece of twaddle." That's what I thought! And then I felt a smarting rebuke. I doubt a week has gone by since when I haven't recalled these words: "See no one in the picture but Jesus. Let Him fill the entire picture of the Christian life." How did Paul put it? "Whatsoever ye do in word or deed, do all in the name of the Lord Jesus." Jesus is everything.

To put it simply, the worldview of the Christian life is seeing no one in the picture but Jesus.

# CHAPTER 5

# A Biblical Worldview
# of Sexuality

*Mark Kelderman*

This book is setting the tone for the view of the world that Christians ought to have regarding various issues and there is none as relevant and important today in our culture as having a biblical worldview of sexuality. In this chapter I want to set before you three major points: (1) Why, as Christians, do we even need to discuss this topic? (2) What are the various worldviews regarding sexuality? (3) What is the beauty and glory of the biblical worldview regarding sexuality.

## Why Discuss Sexuality

The reasons the church needs to address this issue today are many. Take for example the recent decision of the United States Supreme Court regarding same-sex marriage, the interference and intrusion of government in personal convictions of individuals and churches, and the confusion within the church regarding the issues of sexuality. The moral issues of recent decades such as adultery and divorce pale in significance to the issues that face the church and believers today. The views people hold regarding sexuality today are closely connected to the sexual revolution of the '60s and since that time have been compounded by the constant bombardment of sexual issues in the public arena every day. These include homosexuality, transgender issues, polygamy, pornography, and virtual reality sexual relationships. The moral high road that has been touted is "what happens in my bedroom is my business, not yours."

Without hyperbole, the worldview of our culture has been shaped by the so-called scientific study of Dr. Alfred Kinsey. Kinsey authored the *Kinsey Reports* in the late 1940s and early '50s and these became the launching pad for the sexual revolution in the '60s. His views promoted and sanctioned sexual immorality. This study has since been shown to be unscientific and inconclusive. However, by the time his research methodology began to be questioned, the damage had been done in the public arena. People had grown accustomed to the statistic that 1 in 10 people were gay or had inclinations toward that lifestyle. At some points, he even suggested that it was closer to 10–37 percent. However, it is well documented that he conducted his surveys with immoral people, prison inmates, sex offenders, and prostitutes, and even practiced an immoral lifestyle himself and promoted pedophilia.[1]

The significance of this is that SIECUS (Sexuality Information and Education Council of the United States) was launched in 1964 by the Kinsey Institute and soon afterwards sex education was begun in public schools based on the conclusions of this study. This downward spiral of moral decadence has continued as the "scientific acceptability" of this and other so-called scientific studies have entered the public sphere.

The point is that the believer and the church must address these issues today. The call we have been given by God is to bear witness to the truth in this generation. We must address the topic of sexuality not only because it has been forced on us, but we also recognize these issues are not going to disappear. Beside that, when we consider the beauty and glory of biblical sexuality, as understood and promoted by Christians, we realize the world needs to hear about it so that our culture might be transformed by the renewing of their minds. As our culture continues to experience God's judgment, we need to stand united in speaking the truth in love.

If you can just imagine for a moment living ten years from now, what issues do you think your church will be facing? Can a "married" homosexual couple who have come to repentance be received into the church? What would that look like? What counsel is to be given to a same-sex couple who are "married" and one of them has transitioned because of transgender issues? Can the one who has transitioned from female to male serve as an office-bearer of the church? If children have been brought into this relationship, how will the church treat this "marriage" and the children? As you can realize, the need for the church is to be forward-looking rather than

---

1. http://www.drjudithreisman.com/the_kinsey_coverup.html; http://www.dr judithreisman.com/archives/Kinsey_Sex_and_Fraud.pdf

reactionary. We need to wrestle through these issues based on the Word of God.

It is not the point of this short chapter to attempt to address these specific issues but rather to point out the fact that Christians are going to face these issues in churches and families, and therefore we need to begin the dialogue. We must be the salt and light of the world. Just as our Lord ate and drank with publicans and sinners to evangelize them, let's sit down and eat with prostitutes, homosexuals, transgender people, and all kinds of sinners to evangelize them. Let's do this recognizing that we ourselves are sinners. We know that some of us were once engaged in these sins, but we have been washed and cleansed by Christ (1 Cor. 6:9–11) and therefore we must also proclaim the hope there is in Christ for all manner of brokenness.

### Various Worldviews on Sexuality

The second thing we ask is, what kinds of worldviews are there regarding our sexuality? It would be nearly impossible to try to determine the variety of views that people have regarding sexuality and how they explain their views. However, when you take away all the minor details, all the various views regarding sexuality can be broken down into two. When Jesus told the parable of four kinds of places in which seeds were sown, ultimately there were only two results. One produced fruit and all the others did not. It is also true regarding worldviews of sexuality: there are ultimately only two views. One is according to the Word of God and the others are not.

In many ways, all the other views stem in one form or another from what could be called a naturalist view of sex. This view of human sexuality is not different from animal sexuality. It arises from the belief that we have simply evolved and sexuality is nothing more than species preservation and arrives at the logical conclusion that there is no such thing as a moral aspect to sex. People are ultimately concerned with fulfilling personal desires that for the most part do not violate others' rights. People live for the moment. This is a hedonistic view of life, one that encourages that whatever feels good is to be promoted and enjoyed. The other worldview by contrast is vastly different; it is a view that conforms to the Word of God. It is a view that seeks God's plan and purpose in all its practice(s).

One immediately realizes that these two views are diametrically opposed to each other and there is no ground for compromise or agreement. Consider our humanness. The humanistic view does not believe that we are created in the image of God. Therefore, they claim there is no soul or eternal existence and morality is something which has been arrived at by the consensus of the population of the other humans among whom we live. However, those who have the Scripture as their point of reference understand that we are not only created in the image of God but, if we have been born again, we are temples in whom the Spirit of God dwells. And sexuality, being such an intimate and personal act affecting and involving the core of our existence, is practiced in the very presence of God.

Another stark contrast is that the biblical worldview has absolutes; there are areas of sexuality that are not shades of gray. Sexuality is in a different category than our race. To be of a particular skin color is not a moral issue; however, regarding our sexuality, the Bible is very clear there are things that are always right and there are things that are always wrong. What complicates this view is the attempt today by the unbiblical worldview to blur and confuse the issue by speaking about differences of orientation, identity, and practice.

Sadly, what has happened is that those who hold to the biblical worldview and look at sexuality without compromise have been labeled as homophobic or sexophobic. The reality is that we may need to suffer under this title, even if that suffering is for doing good rather than doing evil (1 Pet. 3:17). In other words, as the church we must be known by our actions in reaching out to those who have no hope from the message of the gospel and by sanctifying the Lord God in our hearts.

The challenge we face today is that often these two worldviews have been blurred in the minds and hearts of many believers. Because of this the church has been hindered in proclaiming the gospel to sinners and unable (or unwilling) to take a stand for truth. What the church needs to recover is the beauty of sexuality as God intended it to be.

When I was a student in seminary, we took a course taught by the late Dr. James Grier. For me, this course was transforming in many respects, especially as it related to issues of sexuality. Many of the following thoughts under the third point, the beauty of our sexuality, are those which I have gleaned from his teaching of the subject and from a blog written by Rebecca Capuano.[2]

## The Beauty and Glory of Biblical Sexuality

The challenge we face brings us back to the authority of Scripture. In Genesis we read that God created us in His image, male and female. The unity of our creation images God, while the differences in our creation reflect the images of maleness and femaleness. Often when we speak about male and female, we speak about the roles that these two play. But being male and female is much more than this; it is a life-defining role. It is who you are, defining your being and essence. Being male or female is who you are, not what you do.

This identity of male and female is an expression of the glory of God, while people are the "copy" of the divine. God exists on a completely different level, but in the creation of humankind, God is showing us something of the relationship and being of Himself. God, being three Persons in the one Godhead, lives in a relationship of unity, love, and respect. They do not all do the same things; rather, they have different functions. This being the case, does that make any one Person of the Trinity of more or less value than the others? Of course not. Our culture, however, tells us we get our value from what we do, not from who we are. You are considered of value in our culture if you "come out" or if you identify with who you believe you are and do what you think you should. However, we need to realize that we are not defined by what we do, but who we are *as God created us*.

This idea is important today when people claim that by identifying with something, we actually are that something. There can be no hope and peace in this seeking for identity because it is apart from Christ. The only people who are at peace are those who have not only acknowledged their identity as sinners but who have fled to Christ for pardon and now identify with Him. There are many people, especially in the homosexual and transgender movement, who are crying out for identity. They long to be heard and recognized in their struggles and pain. The truth is that only the believer who hears them understands their cry. This is because they once were

---

2. http://seeluminosity.com/part-1-secular-sex-values-the-new-standard-for-the-world/

crying out as well. It is only the church who can truly help and guide these people to glory. Once I am a believer, then my identity determines my behavior, not the other way around. The fact is that who I am is not based on my feelings but is always based on God's Word.

Many of us, the first question we ask when we meet someone, is, "What do you do?" It subtly indicates that we equate value with function. This would mean our value is based on what we do or accomplish rather than on what God says about us. People today want to identify sexually with how they feel or function, but God has said that in the beginning He made us male and female.[3]

We can say that, because we have been created in the image of God, we have intrinsic value. Another aspect of this having been created as male or female is that we realize that in each gender we reflect something of His nature. Each gender therefore expresses by itself only a partial or an incomplete image of who God is. But, the beauty is that "thru marriage, and sex as an integral part of that, God created the means to join together male and female...so that humans could experience the wholeness of His being. The coming together of male and female in marital sex emulates the union of male and female attributes that encompass the whole of who God is."[4] This is marvelous and beautiful, and yet this idea is being destroyed today in our culture.

God's creation of sex was based on the two genders of male and female and therefore "through these genders, God's nature is revealed and embodied in a tangible way. Gender is not a social construct, or something simply 'chosen.' Gender is a unique, inherent characteristic, with physical, emotional, and spiritual elements, bestowed by God Himself as central to our personhood as made in His image."[5]

Humans were created to be in relationship with God, morally upright and related to God. Man was created to be in relationship to the woman who was not of the earth as was man, but she arose

---

3. We recognize the reality of those who are born intersex. We love them, empathize, and want to offer them hope through the gospel as well. Each one of us experiences the brokenness of our life in our body due to the effect of sin in our world. However, this does not change the original created order and plan of God from the beginning.

4. http://seeluminosity.com/part-5-power-biblical-sex/

5. Ibid.

from man's flesh and bone. So, as Grier said so profoundly, "Your marriage is to be a transcription of the glory of God in this world. People with other worldviews should especially behold God's glory in your marriage and in your sexuality as well." Do you ever wonder why God hates sexual sin so much? It is not so much because sexual sin is a violation of His will but is an assault on the very character of the triune God. Could you imagine for a moment that the Son of God would attach or join Himself in union with any other being than God? To imagine this would be vile and grotesque, yet when we speak about immoral sexual issues this is precisely what we are speaking about. Just as there is a beauty about our sexuality that words cannot begin to describe, so when it is defiled and distorted it should bring about a revulsion of like magnitude. For a man who is in union with his wife to become detached from her and be joined to another is not simply an animalistic and immoral action, it is deeply spiritual. This is not simply a bodily need being met, like our need for water, but it involves our very spirits and souls. We need to realize that God has given to each one of us the right to use our sexual capacity and express this beautiful gift through our wills, but all this according to His Word.

When we read of Adam's creation, it was not the fact that he did not have someone to have sex with that God said, "It is not good," but it was that Adam did not have someone to correspond with him and in this way he did not reflect his Creator. After naming all the animals, even Adam realized there was nothing in all of the created order of living things that corresponded to him. There was no other living thing which had God's image and so God built a woman out of man. And as a reflection of this very act it is said, "Therefore shall a man leave his father and his mother, and shall cleave [be glued] unto his wife." The idea here is ontological, that in their very being, they were to be one. Eve was taken from Adam, she was part of him, she was his wife. A careful reading and comparison of Matthew 19:5 and Genesis 2:24 shows that the one who says "a man [shall] leave his father and his mother, and shall cleave unto his wife" was not Adam but God.

Marriage, therefore, is not about sex but about covenant. It includes all the dimensions of relationship such as love and communication which are far beyond the physical, and all these things come together when the actual physical act of sex takes place. It is the expression of the oneness of these two. Sexuality, then, "is not a picture of an 'act' but on the contrary, it is the picture of an ongoing experience—a dynamic, personal way of being in relationship—in union. The biblical Hebrew expression of sexuality is comprehensive, all-encompassing, thorough, and intimate—involving body, mind, and spirit."[6]

Our culture has sexualized everything to the point that sex is no longer sacred but animalistic. As Grier stated, "We need to desexualize touch and holding and nearness. There is nothing wrong with two men or women crying together, holding one another, loving one another, conversing with one another in deep ways, but there cannot be the consummation of this through the sexual act. That is reserved for marriage of one man and one woman." The act of sex is where spirit touches spirit and heart touches heart and this is why the reality of marriage and its consummation is ultimately found in the relationship of Christ with His church. Here is where we have the beautiful expression of oneness that goes beyond sexuality, where Christ's spirit dwells in our spirits in the most intimate of ways.

This brings us to finally consider the glory of the gospel as it relates to our sexuality. We have a created desire for reality. People are groaning inwardly for this and they do not even realize what they seek. They pursue it in the acts of their sexuality, but they shall forever be disappointed. It is only the new life which is found in Christ that can answer this yearning call and its fruition will ultimately take place in glory. As long as they continue to refuse and reject what God says as truth and refuse to accept who God's Word says they are, they will never live in the joy of this glory.

But those who have found their life in Christ through the gospel are truly alive and in all their brokenness are seeking to live out a life in Christ, in complete dependence on Him and to live for His glory. They repent of their own inclinations and desires, even the predispositions they may have been born with, and choose by grace to live for Him. As you seek to live for the glory of God, for which you have been created, consider this picture. In the Old Testament the place where the worshiper would have met God was in the temple. God made known to His people and to the nations around Israel that He

---

6. http://seeluminosity.com/part-5-power-biblical-sex/

dwelt among His people in the tabernacle and later in the temple. The people of God experienced this presence of God through the mediation of the priest who ministered on their behalf. The minister would go into the holy place with the offering of blood and on behalf of the people he would enter God's presence and would return from that meeting communicating to the people God's blessing and peace.

The place where God was said to dwell was in the Holy of Holies where the ark of the covenant was found. Here was the shekinah glory on display. Here the immaculate holiness of His being shone forth. And, because of this holiness, this place was blocked by a thick veil that separated the most holy place from the rest of the temple. None could come behind that veil and into God's presence except the high priest once a year on the day of atonement. All this was a testimony that sinful people could not enter into God's presence or else they would die. Only through blood was there entrance.

However, our great High Priest, Jesus Christ, changed all this. We are talking about the same holy God as revealed in the Old Testament, and the same separation that exists between this God and a sinful people is a reality. However, what the Old Testament pictured for us in the High Priest is now accomplished through Christ. Christ, having made us priests unto God through His blood, has allowed us immediate access to God Himself. But more than this, Christ has sent His Spirit to dwell within us. We are now the temples of God in this world and this illuminates the glory of what Paul says to the Corinthians, "Know ye not that your bodies are the members of Christ? Shall I then take the members of Christ, and make them the members of an harlot? God forbid. What? Know ye not that he which is joined to an harlot is one body? For two, saith he, shall be one flesh. But he that is joined unto the Lord is one spirit. Flee fornication. Every sin that a man doeth is without the body; but he that committeth fornication sinneth against his own body. What? Know ye not that your body is the temple of the Holy Ghost which is in you, which ye have of God, and ye are not your own? For ye are bought with a price: therefore glorify God in your body, and in your spirit, which are God's" (1 Cor. 6:15–20).

What glory this is! In Christ, we have been united to God Himself; we are one in spirit. What this means is when we, enjoying the bond of a biblical marriage, enter the marriage bed, we are witnessing this unity and the glory of this unity. God rejoices over us in this moment as two, in deepest expressions of love and unity, are joined in one spirit. Does it not become immediately apparent how empty and self-satisfying any other sexual relationship becomes? That is not glory but degradation. Let's not live any longer in that way, but in all we do live for the glory of Him who bought us, body and soul.

## Conclusion

In closing I want to share Thomas Boston's fourfold state of human nature, which can be applied to this exploration of the biblical world-view of sexuality.

1. Innocence – Before the fall, every part of man was perfect, and God said it was good. Man and woman, the way God intended them to be, depicting God perfectly, were united in one flesh in marriage. It was good.

2. Nature – After the fall, every part of man was affected through sin. Sin ruined us—we are now slaves to sin in that we die because of it and we cannot free ourselves from it. All the distortions that bring pain and trouble in our sexual lives is because of this reality. We are under judgment because of it and we pursue our selfish pleasure at the expense of others. We are born with a sinful disposition and live in defiance of God in unbelief and do not seek God's will for our lives. We are hindered from using our gifts (including our sexuality) for His glory.

3. Grace – God has come down into our brokenness and taken sin on Himself in the person of the Son. He bore our sin and took it with Him to the grave and He grants all those who turn to Him deliverance from this bondage to sin and death. This is the beauty of the gospel. There is a response in the heart of sinners to the gospel; having been made alive by the Holy Spirit, we now love God on account of His great love for us. The desires of the renewed sinner are to walk in the way of His commandments and this leads to change. The believer is destined now for the greatest of all pleasures and joys which is to be with Christ and to dwell with God and God in him.

4. Eternal – All this leads us to glory. If we have our minds and hearts focused on this glory, even though we struggle with the effects of sins in our lives, we will never be disappointed in God. We will share in His glory. To God be the glory in everything, including our sexuality.[7]

---

7. Boston, Thomas. *Human Nature in Its Fourfold State : Of Primitive Integrity, Entire Depravity, Begun Recovery, and Consummate Happiness or Misery.* Edinburgh: Banner of Truth Trust, 2002. 1–506.

# CHAPTER 6

# A Christian Worldview
# of Suffering

*Brian Cosby*

---

Immediately after nation-wide tragedies—9/11, tsunamis, floods, mass murders, hurricanes, tornadoes—television and radio programs invite religious leaders from a variety of backgrounds to explain *why* God would allow suffering. Some have said that these events are nothing but "natural phenomena," uncontrolled by a loving God. Others explain that these are direct judgments upon the wickedness of mankind. Still others say that these are all signs of Jesus's impending return. Why *does* God allow suffering? It's a good question.[1]

One of the great tragedies of the American story is the loss of a biblical worldview of suffering, due in part to an ever-increasing belief that joy is only found in the absence of suffering and that we "deserve" health, wealth, and prosperity. We are a nation living from one pleasure high to the next, looking for the next big "wave" that might take us closer and closer toward the sunny sands of the American dream. The American dream has not only become something we pursue, but something we feel we *deserve*. We feel entitled to life, liberty, and continual happiness. But what if the American dream is plunged into a nightmare and dashed to pieces against the rocks of suffering? Is this an "act of God"?

---

1. A portion of this material has been adapted from Brian H. Cosby, *Suffering and Sovereignty: John Flavel and the Puritans on Afflictive Providence* (Grand Rapids: Reformation Heritage Books, 2012). See also Brian Cosby, *A Christian's Pocket Guide to Suffering: How God Shapes Us Through Pain and Tragedy* (Ross-Shire, UK: Christian Focus, 2015); Brian Cosby, "4 Reasons God Ordains Suffering for His People," thegospelcoalition.org (January 8, 2016); Brian Cosby, "Why God Allows His People to Suffer" in *Modern Reformation*, vol. 23, no. 2 (March/April 2014); and Brian Cosby, "Why Does God Ordain Suffering: A Puritan's Answer" in *Evangelical Times* (August 2013).

The effect of this trend is that the church is often like a rudderless boat without direction. The only thing we can think about is dodging the rocks of affliction up ahead or wondering why we've run into so many in the past. And this is why understanding suffering through a coherent, consistent, and biblical worldview is absolutely necessary.

At the outset, though, I need to give a warning. When we consider the reality of suffering, we must not fall into the temptation of diminishing *any* of God's attributes, especially His sovereignty, goodness, or omnipresence. If God is good, but not sovereign, then He doesn't have enough control or power to stop our affliction. While He might be benevolent, He simply could not stop the suffering if He wanted to. If God is sovereign, but not good, then He is simply—God forbid—an unjust, divine bully. And if God were both sovereign and good, but was not everywhere at the same time by His Spirit, then He could not effectively execute His sovereignty and goodness wherever suffering occurs. Thus, we must affirm the manifold and glorious character of our eternal God as He has revealed Himself in His Word.

### The Origin and Types of Suffering

Where did suffering come from? Why do we know death, disease, and dysfunctional relationships all too well? When you observe the world around you, it becomes very clear that there is something very wrong, very evil, in the world. But why?

We know from the Genesis account that God created all things "very good" (Gen. 1:31). He didn't *create* suffering in the beginning. Suffering came as a result of sin, the sin of our first parents, Adam and Eve. God made man—male and female—after His own image to reflect His communicable attributes that they would know life and joy in Him forever. God also gave them an intrinsic freedom of the will to obey Him and His command to not eat of the tree of the knowledge of good and evil.

But they fell. They did *not* obey the Lord their God and fell under the just condemnation of a righteous and holy God. And since Adam represented the whole human race as its federal head, Adam's guilt has been imputed to all his posterity so that even you and I (apart from faith in Christ) are counted "dead in trespasses and sins" and by nature, "children of wrath" (Eph. 2:1, 3).

Immediately, we see the effects of Adam and Eve's fall into sin: *suffering*. Pain in relationships. Pain in childbearing. Pain from work. Pain from thorns and thistles. In fact, the entire creation succumbed to "the bondage of corruption" (Rom. 8:21). Suffering, therefore, came as a curse and effect of the entrance of sin into this world. In one sense, then, it serves as an ongoing and sobering reminder of our rebellious treason against the Creator God.

We experience all kinds of afflictions in this life—external, internal, and even spiritual. While external sufferings can be great indeed,[2] most people agree that internal suffering—especially the grief experienced over the loss of a loved one—is far worse. The pain felt from being separated from someone you love can weigh heavy on the heart and soul. Even Jesus wept at the death of Lazarus (John 11:35).

But there can also be spiritual suffering, which is often brought about by the workings of Satan and his minions. For example, a believer can be oppressed, tempted to despair, tempted to feel abandoned by God, or tempted to feel that he or she remains under condemnation, notwithstanding the finished work of Christ. As the seventeenth-century Puritan Richard Sibbes once noted, "Our disease of body [is] helped by Satan's malice."[3]

### Suffering and the Sovereignty of God

But is God not in absolute control? Does He not declare the end from the beginning (Isa. 46:10)? The answer is an overwhelming "Yes!" God is perfectly and absolutely sovereign. God's sovereignty is expressed, or displayed, in both His eternal decrees and in His day-to-day providences. In other words, God's providence is the execution of His decrees in time and space. Scripture is clear about this. God "worketh *all things* after the counsel of his own will" (Eph. 1:11, emphasis mine). This means that God is also sovereign over suffering. Even God's only begotten Son, our Lord Jesus, was "delivered by the determinate counsel and foreknowledge of God" (Acts 2:23). It was the Lord's will to "bruise him" (Isa. 53:10).

When we read the news reports of hurricanes, tornadoes, and other so-called "natural disasters," we must not give in to a worldview that sees these events occurring apart from the governing hand

---

2. For a list of some of these in the Bible, see 2 Cor. 11:23–33 and Heb. 11:35–38.
3. Richard Sibbes, *The Bruised Reed* (Edinburgh: Banner of Truth Trust, 1998), 57.

of an almighty, omnipotent, and wise God. We do not affirm, like deists, that God simply wound up the clock of creation, only to leave it to work itself out *apart* from His personal and direct governance. Not a chance! We affirm what historically has been referred to as the doctrine of concurrence—that while God has established certain "rules of nature," He *concurrently* guides and directs their every movement.

After Job experienced a devastating series of afflictions to his home and family, Elihu provided an insightful account into the reality that God directly exerts His sovereign will over nature:

> For he saith to the snow, Be thou on the earth; likewise to the small rain, and to the great rain of his strength. He sealeth up the hand of every man; that all men may know his work. Then the beasts go into dens, and remain in their places. Out of the south cometh the whirlwind: and cold out of the north. By the breath of God frost is given: and the breadth of the waters is straitened. Also by watering he wearieth the thick cloud: he scattereth his bright cloud: and it is turned round about by his counsels: that they may do whatsoever he commandeth them upon the face of the world in the earth. He causeth it to come, whether for correction, or for his land, or for mercy. (Job 37:6–13)

God is in absolute control over every wind, every tornado, every molecule, and every sparrow that falls to the ground (Matt. 10:29).

Before we consider the pressing question of *why* God ordains suffering, we need to clear the air over the reality of God's sovereignty and the presence of evil in this world. To be sure, suffering and evil are not the same. They are often linked together, but suffering in and of itself is not morally evil. It would be rather odd, for example, for Paul to say that we "glory in tribulations" (Rom. 5:3) if those tribulations were morally wicked.

So how does God relate to evil? While it is beyond the scope and purpose of this chapter to give any decent explanation of this, let me summarize this by saying that God *permits* evil (e.g., the story of Job, the "messenger of Satan" in 2 Cor. 12:7, etc.), *restrains* evil (e.g., Gen. 20:6), and *overrules* evil and sin (e.g., Gen. 50:20) for His good purposes. Thus, God cannot be charged as the author of evil. His glory is magnified by His actions of permitting, restraining, and overruling evil, even though we don't always understand how or why. Indeed, "The secret things belong unto the LORD our God: but those things which are revealed belong unto us and to our children for ever" (Deut. 29:29).

When asked about why a certain man was born blind—whether it was because of his own sin or his parents' sin—Jesus told His disciples, "Neither hath this man sinned, nor his parents: but that the works of God should be made manifest in him" (John 9:3). We must come before these weighty matters of God's sovereignty and suffering with a right awe and reference of a holy God who works all things together for good "to them that love God, to them who are the called according to his purpose" (Rom. 8:28).

## Why Does God Ordain Suffering?

It might be tempting to read the motives of God's mysterious providence *into* the events of our lives, but we need to be careful about doing this. Just because you stub your toe on a chair doesn't necessarily mean that God is punishing you for not reading your Bible earlier that morning. Conversely, if you receive a raise at work (or some other benefit), it doesn't necessarily mean that God is blessing you because you sent "seed money" to a flashy TV preacher (by the way, please don't do this!).

So why does God ordain suffering? Under the banner of God's glory, sufferings come (1) as raw effects of God's just judgment and wrath *for the unbelieving world* and (2) paternal disciplines *for the believer in Christ.* For the one who continues in his rebellion and unbelief against God, suffering comes as the unmitigated, unsanctified judgment of God—in part in this life, and in fullness in the life to come.

But for the one who has faith in Christ, suffering comes in a different vein, namely, the blood-vein of Jesus. The English Puritan John Flavel wrote that suffering for the Christian is a *sanctified* affliction: "Behold, then, a sanctified affliction is a cup, whereinto Jesus hath wrung and pressed the juice and virtue of all his mediatorial offices. Surely, that must be a cup of generous, royal wine, like that in the supper, a cup of blessing to the people of God."[4]

Though there are certainly more, here are five biblical reasons why God ordains various "sanctified afflictions" for His people.

---

4. John Flavel, *Navigation Spiritualized* in *The Works of John Flavel*, 6 vols. (Edinburgh: Banner of Truth Trust, 1968), 5:252.

First, God ordains suffering in the life of the believer *to kill sin and produce godliness*. God will often use suffering to reveal to us the sin that clings closely to our hearts. The Reformers and post-Reformers would often call these "searching afflictions" because they tend to seek out and reveal the sin that lies dormant. Sin is often like a sleeper cell and will awaken at the fire of affliction. When we suddenly come upon a trial or tribulation, our pride, impatience, or unbelief will often surface.

When this happens, I am able to recognize it, confess it, repent of it, and abide all the more in the true Vine. And so suffering serves to deter the believer from greater sin, like a would-be thief considering his suffering *in prison* before stealing. Suffering serves as a cleanser to reveal our sin and deter us from greater sin so that we might put to death the deeds of the flesh. And as we die to sin, we are called to live unto Christ. Richard Sibbes remarked, "We need bruising so that reeds may know themselves to be reeds, and not oaks. Even reeds need bruising, by reason of the remainder of pride in our nature, and to let us see that we live by mercy."[5]

Sometimes, suffering comes upon a community of faith, a local church, for these same reasons. During communal times of affliction, the saints of God are often drawn together to bear one another's burdens (Gal. 6:2) and to spur one another on to holiness, even as "iron sharpeneth iron" (Prov. 27:17). Thomas Watson wrote, "Afflictions are the medicine that God uses to carry off our spiritual diseases."[6]

Second, God ordains suffering in the life of the believer *so that he might relinquish the temporal and lay hold of the eternal*. God uses suffering to wean us from an over-love of this world and redirect our thoughts and affections for that which is eternal: "Set your affection on things above, not on things on the earth" (Col. 3:2). Sometimes God will take away our earthly treasures for our heavenly good.

We are prone to take God's good gifts and elevate them above the giver, which is idolatry. Afflictions may strip us of these gifts so that we might say, "God is enough for me"; so that we might see *God*—not His gifts—as the greatest treasure in the universe. As insensitive as

---

5. Sibbes, *The Bruised Reed*, 5.
6. Thomas Watson, *All Things for Good* (Edinburgh: Banner of Truth Trust, 1986), 29.

this might sound, God might even take away precious children so that we might learn a deeper dependence upon Him.

A Christian worldview of suffering, then, would place Christians as "strangers and pilgrims" (1 Peter 2:11) in this world, journeying onward toward the celestial city. Our citizenship is in heaven (Phil. 3:20) and we await our Savior from there. Even though we are *in* the world, we are not *of* it (John 17:14). Sometimes we cling too tightly to that which withers and fades away—"where moth and rust doth corrupt, and where thieves break through and steal" (Matt. 6:19). Suffering will often remind us of our place in this world and, as we behold God as our great treasure (as the old hymn says), "the things of earth will grow strangely dim, in the light of His glory and grace."[7]

Third, God ordains suffering in the life of the believer *to produce a sincere faith, devoid of hypocrisy*. The Bible frequently speaks of God's people being refined like gold through the fire of affliction. Jeremiah writes, "Therefore thus saith the LORD of hosts, Behold, I will melt them, and try them" (Jer. 9:7). Likewise, God tells Zechariah, "And I will bring the third part through the fire, and will refine them as silver is refined, and will try them as gold is tried" (Zech. 13:9). Speaking of the Lord's coming, Malachi writes, "And he shall sit as a refiner and purifier of silver...that they may offer unto the LORD an offering in righteousness" (Mal. 3:3).

When suffering comes, it often has the effect of distinguishing the true believer and the hypocrite by the response of each. In suffering, we are given the opportunity to discover the sincerity of our love, hope, and faith in God. You could lose your job, your wife, or your children, and still say—in the midst of the deepest, darkest pain—"God is still enough." Is that insensitive? With all humility, we must say, "no." Our refuge and fortress becomes so much more so—at least in our experience of Him—in the midst of our darkest days.

Churches around the world are experiencing intense suffering, often through persecution. To a lesser extent this happens in America (though that might be changing in the coming years). During these trials, the Lord often sifts the visible church, revealing what John Flavel called Jesus's "summer friends"[8]—those who belonged to the church because of prestige or other worldly motives, and leave

---

7. Helen H. Lemmel, "Turn Your Eyes Upon Jesus," 1922.
8. Flavel, *Preparation for Sufferings*, in *The Works of John Flavel*, 6:18.

because they were never truly regenerated (cf. 1 John 2:19). Affliction will often cause the believer to cling to God and the unbeliever to become increasingly hard-hearted. In this way, suffering serves as a sort of test or trial, separating the sheep from the goats, the wheat from the tares. Thomas Watson wrote, "God takes away the world, that the heart may cleave more to him in sincerity."[9]

Fourth, God ordains suffering in the life of the believer so that *he or she might bear witness to the watching world.* Under the rod of affliction, we are given opportunity to bear witness to the reality of the power of the gospel in our lives to an observant and anti-God world—which has often caused those same observers to repent and trust in Christ! The hope of the believer in God shines bright when he or she faces affliction.

We are told to "sorrow not, even as others which have no hope" (1 Thess. 4:13). But a side effect of this not-giving-in-to-a-no-hope disposition is a witness to those observing you in your trial. I have seen many saints suffer so well that non-believers are left in a state of awe and wonder at the indelible peace exhibited. Our frequent trials prove that our hope and faith are not in vain, but rather serve as an occasion to demonstrate the reality of the gospel.

Fifth, God ordains suffering in the life of the believer so that he or she *might cultivate deeper fellowship with God through the ordinary means of grace: His Word, prayer, and the sacrament of the Lord's Supper.* The prophet Hosea writes, "Come, let us return unto the LORD: for he hath torn, and he will heal us" (Hos. 6:1). Indeed, as we experience suffering at the sovereign and loving hand of God, we are to cultivate communion and fellowship with Jesus Christ, the greatest Sufferer.

In this way, we know the "fellowship of his sufferings" (Phil. 3:10). This was the apostle Peter's instruction: "Beloved, think it not strange concerning the fiery trial which is to try you, as though some strange thing happened unto you: but rejoice, inasmuch as ye are partakers of Christ's sufferings; that, when his glory shall be revealed, ye may be glad also with exceeding joy" (1 Peter 4:12–13). When we experience suffering, we are driven to cling to our rock, refuge, and fortress—the true and living God. Indeed, "God is our refuge and strength, a very present help in trouble" (Ps. 46:1). Or, "Cast thy burden upon the LORD, and he shall sustain thee" (Ps. 55:22). How do we

---

9. Watson, *All Things for Good*, 28.

practically go about entrusting ourselves and cultivating communion with God under trial? We do this ordinarily through His Word, through prayer, and through the sacrament of the Lord's Supper.

These are just a few of the ways in which the Lord sanctifies us through His paternal discipline and chastisement. In the moment, it's difficult to see these as effects of His loving care, just as any child would have difficulty understanding the love during his or her parental discipline. But a Christian worldview of suffering must see the trials and sufferings in our lives coming from a sovereign, good, and omnipresent God who loves His people, in Christ, and who will finish the good work that He began in them (Phil. 1:6).

## Rightly Responding to Suffering

Please take this in the right way, but our suffering does not give us the justifying excuse to sin. Sin is never justified. Just because I suffer doesn't give me the license to act in wicked ways. John Flavel wrote: "Thou hast more reason to lament thy dead heart, than thy dead friend…. To lose the heavenly warmth and spiritual liveliness of thy affections, is undoubtedly a far more considerable loss, than to lose the wife of thy bosom, or the sweetest child that ever a tender parent laid in the grave."[10] He added, "The least sin is more formidable to you than the greatest affliction: doubtless you would rather choose to bury all your children than provoke and grieve your heavenly Father."[11] The reality, as hard as this might be, is that ultimately what makes a person truly miserable it not suffering, but sin. In fact, sin increases the sting of suffering.

Jesus is so much more than a mere example for us, but He *is* nevertheless an example! As the apostle Peter exhorts, "For even hereunto were ye called: because Christ also suffered for us, leaving us an example, that ye should follow his steps" (1 Peter 2:21). We should respond rightly to suffering, which can be both *passive* and *active* responses. Passively, we can rest and trust in the sovereignty of God, that He is working out His will with all wisdom and grace and justice. Passively, we can say with the psalmist, "It is good for

---

10. Flavel, *A Token for Mourners*, in *The Works of John Flavel*, 5:619.

11. Flavel, *A Token for Mourners*, 5:626. Similarly, he wrote, "Suffering is but a *respective, external*, and *temporal* evil; but sin is an universal, internal, and everlasting evil" (Flavel, *Preparation for Sufferings*, 6:63).

me that I have been afflicted; that I might learn thy statutes" (Ps. 119:71). Or, with Job, "The LORD gave, and the LORD hath taken away; blessed be the name of the LORD" (Job 1:21).

Active responses might include: (1) communing with God by reading and meditating upon His Word, (2) individual and corporate prayer, (3) resting in the assurance of His promises through the Lord's Supper, (4) reading helpful literature on the topic of suffering, (5) repenting of any particular sin that has become evident during your trial, (6) serving others as a follower of the Suffering Servant, and (7) intentional fellowship in your local church through corporate worship, small groups, or discipleship. These are ways, as the Puritans would say, to "improve" upon your sufferings. Don't waste them. Let your response to suffering reflect a worldview that sees suffering in its right perspective.

### Ministering to Sufferers

Before we conclude, I'd like to give you just a few things to consider when you minster to those experiencing suffering and hardship.

First, *be quick to listen.* When sufferers are in the throes of their affliction, giving them a seven-point outline of a biblical theology of suffering might not be the best timing. They might need for you to just sit with them and listen to them. They might need you to simply show them that you love them. And that's a good thing. Sure, speak the truth in love, but know *when* to speak! One shouldn't always head into a situation with the predetermined plan of outlining the finer points of how God is glorified in people's pain. Just love them by listening to and being with them in their suffering

Second, *restrain the urge to give sufferers empty platitudes.* Phrase such as, "Oh, this isn't so bad" or "Just look on the bright side" or the like don't help. Listen and strive to sympathize with them.

Third, *point them and lead them to the means of grace: God's Word, prayer, and the sacraments.* If they are going to grow in and through their suffering, it will ordinarily be through the ordinary means that God has ordained to sanctify His people. But walk with them in these areas. Offer to bring them to church, pray with and for them, and show them the wonderful gift of the Lord's Table—that Jesus, by His Spirit, nourishes our faith and helps us see His sin-atoning suffering for us.

Fourth, *follow through with the community of faith*. Oftentimes, churches do well providing prayer and meals during the first week of a sufferer's trial, but then neglect them afterwards. Follow through. If someone in your church is experiencing affliction, continue to minster to them with care, comfort, support, and any physical and spiritual needs they may have. Also, many sufferers tend toward isolation in the midst of their suffering. Bring them in. Include them in the fellowship of the saints and Lord's Day worship.

In all of this, may we look to Christ, our suffering servant, who came not to be served, but to serve and to give His life as a ransom for many (Mark 10:45). The writer of Hebrews reminds us, "For we have not an high priest which cannot be touched with the feeling of our infirmities; but was in all points tempted like as we are, yet without sin" (Heb. 4:15). In our suffering, we may commune with Christ who drank the cup of affliction to its bitter end, so that we might enjoy the sweet cup of blessing, which runneth over. Jesus knows your pain, your trials, your temptations, and your sufferings because He's been there too. And He will never leave you nor forsake you.

## Conclusion

I want to close by giving you a portion of the words of the well-known hymn, "How Firm a Foundation," probably written by Robert Keen in 1787. May God grant you grace to see this reality of suffering through the lens of His holy Word.

> How firm a foundation, ye saints of the Lord,
> Is laid for your faith in His excellent Word!
> What more can He say than to you He hath said,
> You, who unto Jesus for refuge have fled?
>
> Fear not, I am with thee, O be not dismayed,
> For I am thy God and will still give thee aid;
> I'll strengthen and help thee, and cause thee to stand
> Upheld by My righteous, omnipotent hand.
>
> When through the deep waters I call thee to go,
> The rivers of woe shall not thee overflow;
> For I will be with thee, thy troubles to bless,
> And sanctify to thee thy deepest distress.

When through fiery trials thy pathways shall lie,
My grace, all sufficient, shall be thy supply;
The flame shall not hurt thee; I only design
Thy dross to consume, and thy gold to refine.

The soul that on Jesus has leaned for repose,
I will not, I will not desert to its foes;
That soul, though all hell should endeavor to shake,
I'll never, no never, no never forsake.

# FLAMING TRUTHS FOR THE CHRISTIAN'S ZEAL

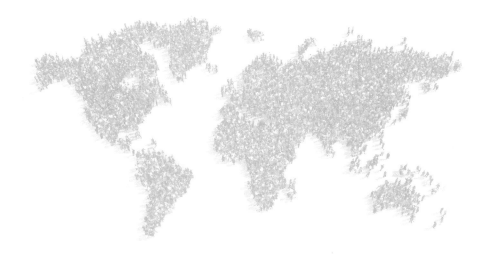

# CHAPTER 7

# Joyful Exiles:
# A Worldview for Pilgrims
1 Peter 1:1–9

*Charles M. Barrett*

---

The Christian worldview is not merely a set of ideas or doctrines detached from daily living. Any worldview shapes how a person understands and interprets the world and governs actions in this life.[1] For one to embrace a properly called Christian worldview there needs to be more than mental assent to certain doctrines. There needs to be a supernatural transformation of the entire person: mind, will, and affections. A person needs to be a Christian. This transformation occurs by God's grace seen in His Trinitarian work of redemption.

A worldview that limits its focus or attention on what is seen by only the physical eye will invariably lead to a materialistic outlook. As Christians, by God's grace, our view of the world is shaped foremost by what we see by faith according to God's Word. God's Word shapes and informs how we view this life and the way we live. Through God's Word the Christian understands that a proper worldview encompasses more than just the present age. It extends prior to creation when only God existed. For God is the ultimate reality. It also extends to the new heavens and new earth, to an eternal inheritance that does not fade away.

---

1. James Anderson, *What's Your Worldview* (Wheaton, Ill.: Crossway, 2014), 12. Anderson defines a worldview as "an all-encompassing perspective on everything that exists and matters to us." James Sire, *The Universe Next Door* (Downers Grove, Ill.: IVP Academic, 2009), 20. Sire defines it as "a commitment, a fundamental orientation of the heart…that we hold (consciously or subconsciously) about the basic constitution of reality, and that provides the foundation on which we live and move and have our being." Albert Wolters, *Creation Regained: Biblical Basics for a Reformational Worldview* (Grand Rapids: Eerdmans, 1985). Wolters describes a worldview as "the comprehensive framework of one's basic beliefs about things."

Though the entirety of Scripture is foundational to how we are to view the world around us, Peter's first letter provides the Christian with the broad framework of a sound worldview. In the opening verses of his letter, the apostle writes about the main subjects that a worldview considers: God, identity, sin and its solution, suffering and its purpose, and where we go after this life. Peter focuses on who God is in order to encourage Christians to understand who they are and how they are to live in this world. By doing so Peter affords believers with one of the most significant portions of Scripture to guide and direct how we understand the world in which we live and how we interact with the surrounding culture. Miroslav Volf stated, 1 Peter is "one text which speaks more pointedly and comprehensively to the problem of 'Christ and culture' than any other in the New Testament."[2] In doing so, it delivers a summary of the Christian worldview.

### The God Who Is, Is the God Who Redeems (1:1–2)

Peter begins his letter describing his readers as "elect," strangers of the Dispersion (1:1). Understanding your identity is necessary to properly understand the world around you. We all stand in a particular relationship to this world. Every person is either an alien to God and at home in this world (Eph. 2:12), or a child of God and a stranger to this world (1 Peter 1:1). Peter immediately draws attention to a believer's status as elect of God and stranger to this world.

The idea of *stranger* is two-fold. First, God's people are not made for this world. Their alien status points to their citizenship of an eternal home, the residence to which they belong and toward which they are moving in this pilgrim life (1:4). Second, the idea of *stranger* signifies the tension a Christian experiences while living in this present evil age. A mindset exists in an unbelieving culture that is opposed to the holy life believers are to live (1:14–16). Whether speaking in terms of citizenship or ethics, a Christian is just not at home in this world.[3] Rather than discouraging his readers at the outset by reminding them that they are strangers scattered through the world, Peter intends to encourage them by focusing on the God who redeems.

---

2. Miroslav Volf, *Captive to the Word of God: Engaging the Scriptures for Contemporary Theological Reflection* (Grand Rapids: Eerdmans, 2010), 67.

3. Karen H. Jobes, *1 Peter*, Baker Exegetical Commentary on the New Testament (Grand Rapids: Baker Academic, 2005), 61.

The apostle directs the Christian's attention to the work of the triune God. Our redemption is the work of God, who is one God in three Persons. Three prepositional phrases in verse 2 describe the particular work of the Persons of the Godhead. We are elect, or chosen: 1) "according to the foreknowledge of God the Father," 2) "through sanctification of the Spirit," and 3) "unto obedience and sprinkling of the blood of Jesus Christ." Each reference to the Person is subjective, stressing that every aspect of redemption is the work of God.

### According to the Foreknowledge of God the Father

God the Father set His sovereign, electing love upon Christians. The reason a Christian lives as a stranger and foreigner in this life rests upon the gracious act of God the Father. We are not aliens because some tyrant despot forced us from our homes. Rather, we are aliens and strangers in this life because God chose us for Himself. Your status flows from the loving and all-wise plan of God the Father. Foreknowledge entails more than knowing events or people before they happen. Foreknowledge encompasses the wise and loving purpose of a sovereign God to rescue sinners through the life, death, and resurrection of Jesus Christ.[4] Foreknowledge involves the way in which God redeems (Acts 2:23, 1 Peter 1:20), as well as those who are redeemed (Rom. 8:29, 1 Peter 1:1–2).

The marvelous reality of grace opens wide when we consider when election according to the Father's foreknowledge occurred. He set His love upon us before the foundation of the world (Eph. 1:4). We were not always strangers to this world. In fact, in our sin we loved the world and our own former lusts (1 Peter 1:14), malice, guile, hypocrisies, envies, and evil words (2:1). Yet, from His own will and good pleasure God foreordained that His own Son shed His blood to redeem and rescue us from our sins (1:18–20). God in His grace opened our eyes to believe (1:21) and opened our mouths that we might taste (2:3) the goodness of His salvation. As you sojourn through this life, amid all its opposition and hostility, you go with the comfort and confidence that you are what you are because the Father chose you according to His sovereign plan. As a wise and

---

4. Simon J. Kistemaker and William Hendriksen, *Exposition of the Epistles of Peter and the Epistle of Jude*, vol. 16, New Testament Commentary (Grand Rapids: Baker, 1953–2001), 35–36.

loving Father, God wills for you to be a stranger in this life that you may know your eternal home with Him in the next.

Peter does not write about election in order to be controversial or speculative. Nowhere in Scripture is this doctrine presented as such. Peter immediately draws our attention to this doctrine so that we might find comfort. The epistle begins and ends with election to remind Christians of the loving Fatherhood of God through Christ (1:1; 5:13). What great comfort! Though this world opposes you, and although you are homesick for your eternal destiny, you are not left alone. You are chosen. Your pilgrimage to your eternal home is established by the eternal plan of God the Father.

### Through Sanctification of the Spirit

Your election according to the Father's foreknowledge before time is brought about in time by the sanctifying work of the Holy Spirit. All whom the Father chooses the Spirit sets apart. The means by which God works faith in the believer's life is the Holy Spirit. The Holy Spirit's ministry and influence upon Christians center on setting them apart for God's purpose and to conform them to the image of Jesus Christ by making them holy. Peter furthers the idea of sanctification as purification, recalling the Old Testament imagery of consecration (1:22).

Because Christians have been set apart, or sanctified, by the Spirit, the pilgrim's life ought to be characterized by a new way of living. Christians are strangers in this world because the Spirit has set us apart from this world. There is a new way of life. God redeemed Christians from their former and vain conversation, or way of life (1:18). Peter's theme of strangers and purity appears again in chapter 2. Peter pleads with Christians as strangers and pilgrims to abstain from fleshly lusts (2:11). The remaining corruption in the believer's life opposes his status and identity as one chosen of God and set apart. Peter writes that these fleshly lusts war against the soul. This warfare language only heightens the tension Christians experience in this world as they await their reward. Yet, they rest assured and comforted that the Spirit has set them apart and is continually working in them according to the purpose of God the Father.

*Unto Obedience and Sprinkling of the Blood of Jesus Christ*

The final prepositional phrase in the Trinitarian work of redemption leads us to the heart of the gospel. We have been chosen according to the foreknowledge of God the Father, set apart by the Holy Spirit, and redeemed by the work of Jesus Christ. Jesus, the Son of God incarnate, redeems us by His perfect obedience and His shed blood. As he does throughout his epistle, Peter utilizes Old Testament imagery to highlight the work of redemption. In the Old Testament the people of God responded to the covenant by pledging obedience. Moses then sprinkled them with blood (Ex. 24:3–8). Humanity, however, fails in offering a perfect obedience and the sacrifices of the older covenant could never cleanse in themselves. Jesus Christ fulfills both the obedience necessary to be right with God, as well as accomplishes the payment for our sins. We have not been redeemed with corruptible things, but with the precious blood of Christ, who earned the right to be *the* sacrificial lamb because He was without blemish and without spot (1:18–19).

It can be discouraging wandering through this world as aliens and strangers. But to claim an identity as merely strangers in this world is only half the story. We are strangers to be sure; but what is more, we are blood-bought saints marching on toward our heavenly home. Christians do not fully grasp their identity apart from understanding the God who redeems them. As Peter directs their attention preeminently toward God to better understand their identity and the world around them he leads them to the gospel. If someone were to ask you your worldview, how long would it take before you get to the gospel of Jesus Christ? The apostle considers it to be the center point of the Christian's worldview. God, in His Trinitarian work of redemption, grounds the Christian in this life and shapes the way we interpret events in this world.

## The God Who Is, Is the God Who Keeps (1:3–7)

Peter extends our understanding of God to see Him as One who keeps and guards all those He redeems. God does not leave His people to navigate through life on their own. Not only does He not abandon them, He completely transforms their lives, giving them hope through the resurrection of Jesus Christ. According to His abundant mercy God begets Christians, quickens and makes them alive, unto a living hope by the resurrection of Jesus Christ from the dead (1:3). The great miracle and reality of Christ's resurrection radically changes how we interpret the world around us. God redeems us through the precious blood of Jesus and makes us alive through the resurrection. The victory of Jesus Christ over sin, death, and the Devil fills the believer with hope in this life.

Many people search and long for hope in this life. Hope is closely tied to meaning and it can only truly be known in union with Christ. People desperately grasp for meaning and purpose only to discover frustration and emptiness apart from Christ. While this world provides many good things, the good things of this world cannot satisfy if we seek them apart from God. The proper enjoyment of created things is to lead us to love the Creator of things (Ps. 104). Pursuing the gifts apart from the One who gave breeds only frustration and emptiness. Our hope is in the living God (1 Tim. 4:10). Peter brings us to the basis for our hope, namely, the living Christ. This hope prevails through the most difficult trials of life. The hope prevails through life's trials, not by our own strength, but by God's faithfulness to keep, safeguard, and preserve both our inheritance and us.

### He Keeps an Inheritance that Fadeth Not Away

God makes us alive "to an inheritance incorruptible, and undefiled, and that fadeth not away, reserved [kept] in heaven for you" (1:4). The three descriptors of our inheritance vividly picture the excellency of the Christian's eternal reward. Our inheritance cannot be destroyed, defiled, or diminished. It is eternal, pure, and beautiful.[5] And by God's grace it is ours.

How different this is from earthly inheritances. Inheritances in this life can be corrupted by the greed of the inheritors. An earthly inheritance can be wasted quickly and run out. And earthly heirlooms often retain a sentimental value that far outlasts the beauty of the piece itself. Not only are earthly inheritances subject to these things, they must be split between the heirs. Not every heir can receive the fullness of the inheritance. Yet, each child of God receives the same fullness of the eternal inheritance kept in heaven for us.

There is another contrast between earthy inheritances and our heavenly inheritance. Earthly inheritances generally follow the death

---

5. Kistemaker and Hendriksen, *1 Peter*, 43.

of a loved one. Someone dies and we receive an inheritance. Sure, you get stuff, but you lose the person. The full receiving of our heavenly inheritance also means the full receiving of Jesus Christ. He earned an inheritance for us with His perfect life, sacrificial death, and triumphal resurrection. God keeps this inheritance for us and we come into it at the glorious appearing of our Lord and Savior Jesus Christ (1:7). Our inheritance is kept until the full and final reunion of Christians with their Savior.

### He Keeps Us for Heaven

Peter encourages Christians not only by drawing their attention to the grace of God in keeping our inheritance for us, but also by comforting them that God keeps us as well. It is a wonderful truth to know that the future is certain. But we live in the here and now in the midst of hardships and trials. Doubts arise not so much regarding whether heaven will be kept, but whether we will make it to heaven. So, Peter assures us that we, too, are being kept by the power of God through faith unto salvation ready to be revealed at the last time (1:5). Richard Sibbes wrote, "He that keeps heaven for us, keeps us for heaven, till he have put us into possession of it."[6]

This is where Peter's pastoral heart and personal experience shine for the reader. We can almost see him writing these words of comfort as he reflects on God's power to keep him through his own life's trials. On that night before the Lord Jesus gave His life as a ransom for many He gathered His disciples and warned them of Satan's desire to have them and sift them as wheat (Luke 22:31–34). He singled Peter out and alerted him to Satan's focused attack on him and his eventual denial. Peter, however, rested in his own strength. His worldview at that time failed to take into account the complexity of the trials he would face. He announced his faithful commitment to Christ, sure that he would be willing to go both to prison and to death for Christ's sake.

The Lord as the Good Shepherd prayed for Peter that his faith would not fail and that he would be restored. Peter's faith, because of his three denials, took a beating that night. The despondency and discouragement ran deep in the next few days as the Lord was

---

6. Richard Sibbes, *The Complete Works of Richard Sibbes*, ed. Alexander Balloch Grosart, vol. 1 (Dublin: James Nichol; W. Robertson, 1862), 326.

crucified, died, and was buried. The risen Lord, according to His abundant mercy, restored the apostle and commissioned him to feed His sheep (John 21:15–17). Peter's faith remained unbroken by the power of God according to the intercessory ministry of Jesus Christ.

Now with a more mature worldview, Peter encourages and assures Christians that they, too, will make it through their pilgrimage kept by God's power. Though now for a time they are in heaviness through manifold temptations and trials, the Christian will persevere (1 Peter 1:6). God keeps His people through fiery trials. He describes these as manifold. Many types and kinds of trials afflict believers in this life. Whether they are trials in mind or body, regarding marriage or children, at work, or involving hostility from believers, all have a trying and testing effect on faith. Added to these trials "the devil, as a roaring lion, walketh about, seeking whom he may devour" (5:8).

The fiery testing of our faith conforms us to Christ. Throughout Peter's letter he points us to Christ, who endured testing and affliction. Just as Christ experienced His own glorification at the end of His suffering, so we will be found unto praise and honor and glory at the appearing of Jesus Christ (1:7). The means by which we see such an end is the power of God that keeps us and guards us. This pilgrim life is no easy trek. But God guides us all the way, protecting and preserving us to the very end. As we consider the circumstances of life we do so with faith in the God who keeps both our inheritance and us.

### The God Who Is, Is the God Who Delights (1:8–9)

Through this opening section of his epistle, Peter addresses difficult matters of trials, temptations, and fire. He describes real-life experiences that weigh upon, and even grieve, the believer. But he focuses on God. God redeems and God keeps. But God also delights. What is surprising in this opening is not the hard realities of our pilgrimage, but the emphasis on our affections. He calls us to love, to trust, and to rejoice. These affections in life's trials find their objects only in the God who delights.

*Loving God*

Peter saw Jesus in the flesh, but he knows that his readers have not. What they do see with their physical eyes is what causes distress in this life. He directs them to realities that cannot be seen, but are greater than the trials they face. You cannot see God with your physical eyes, but you know Him and you love Him. In this pilgrimage, love the God who first loved you. He redeemed you. Fix your gaze upon the One who gave His life for you and redeemed you by His blood. Lift your eyes to the One who washed away your sins. Love the One who set you apart and is at work in you. As a child loves his father, so love the Father who chose you and adopted you into His family. These truths must shape and govern your worldview; they must govern your affections. Even when the world reproaches you, know that "the spirit of glory of and God resteth upon you" (4:14). As you meditate upon the work of God in your life, the great outpouring of His grace and mercy, you will find that your heart grows in love for the God who loves you.

### Trusting God

Circumstances of life may lead you to doubt the promises and goodness of God. Yet, by His grace you trust. You believe in His purposes for you. You may not understand all the ways of God and how He is accomplishing His will in you. Your faith is tried with fire and it may burn and hurt. You see the fire but not His hand. Dear Christian, continue believing because He is at work and the trial is necessary (1:6). The God who brings you through the trial is the God who keeps you in the trial. He is good and He is trustworthy. God never disappoints. Just because you cannot see Him does not mean He is absent. We know the experience of Asaph all too well. Though it seems that our feet are almost gone and our steps have well-nigh slipped, nevertheless God has held our right hand and we are continuously with Him (Ps. 73:2, 23). We trust the God who holds us and keeps us.

### Rejoicing in God

Peter calls us to rejoice even in the midst of trials (1:6). He exhorts us to lovingly and trustingly rejoice with joy unspeakable (1:8). Our rejoicing is not because we are in the trial, nor is it a rejoicing at the trial. He says, "*wherein* ye greatly rejoice" (v. 6, emphasis added). We rejoice in the reality that we have been born again to a living hope and an eternal inheritance, and because we are kept. The rejoicing is in God Himself and His sovereign purpose in us to save us and to bring us home. As we consider the great glories of salvation we experience a joy that cannot even be expressed in words. We rejoice with a joy that is full of glory. This joy is deeply rooted in our union with Christ and the communion we have with the triune God (John 15:11). Our unspeakable joy flows from our present experience of salvation, as well as the future hope of our full salvation (1 Peter 1:9).

We will one day receive the end of our faith, namely, the salvation of our souls. The end of our faith is the beginning of sight. Just because we have not seen Him and just because we do not see Him now does not mean that we never will. There will be a revelation of Jesus Christ that exceeds our comprehension and our present vocabulary (1:13). The salvation of our souls brings an end to our pilgrimage and a beginning to our eternal rest. One day we will be home. Our salvation is certain. Such a future certainty brings about a present joy. This life is hard. It is a pilgrimage. We pilgrim through this life of trials as joyful exiles chosen, set apart, redeemed, and kept by God.

# CHAPTER 8

# Conforming Our Worldview to the Great Commission

*Gerald Bilkes*

If you have ever had your eyes tested, you have had the experience of sitting in the ophthalmologist's chair with a vision chart at some distance. This chart, also known as a Snellen chart, was developed by the Dutch scientist Hermann Snellen in 1862 to test vision acuity, or accuracy of vision. If so, perhaps you can relate to the experience—sitting in a dark room, peering into the distance at a few letters illuminated on the wall, first with one eye covered, then with the other eye covered, struggling to make out whether that symbol you see is an E or an F, an M or an N, a B or a D.

Whether or not you have ever had your eyes checked, we all need to have our worldview tested. A worldview operates much like a pair of glasses or contact lenses, which help us to see things around us accurately. Every one of us has a worldview, whether we have ever stopped to think it through or not. And, just as a pair of glasses following a faulty prescription will make you see the world in a faulty way, so a faulty worldview causes us to see this world, and life in it, inaccurately.

When Adam, the first man and our federal head, sinned against God in the garden of Eden, he (and we with him) bought into and took on a worldview promoted by Satan himself. It is a view that is at odds with God, and in rebellion against Him. It goes against His Word and the truths of it.

Those who have been regenerated by the Spirit of God have had their outlook on the world corrected. They now see the kingdom of God (John 3:3). Even they, however, continue to need instruction from God's Word, and the influence of God's Spirit. The world, the devil, and our own natural minds continue to pull us toward a natural and carnal view of this world, one that flatters us and indulges us and loosens us from the claims of God's Word. Twenty-four hours a day, the media, politicians, academics, "superstars," and sports heroes of this world bombard us with their spectacles. They say, as it were: "Here, try these. Here, try this. Here, look at things this way." How desperately we need, as Paul says, to be "transformed by the renewing of [our] mind" (Rom. 12:2).

Part of this transformation of our mind involves conforming our worldview to the Great Commission found in Matthew 28:18–20. In other words, if we have a worldview that doesn't take account of the Great Commission, no matter how biblical it seems to be in other ways, there is something missing, and we need, by the power of the Holy Spirit, to have our worldview conformed to the truth of the whole Word of God. This worldview is so basic that it comprises the final words of the first gospel, Matthew, formulated as it is there as a manifesto belonging to all those who believe the gospel. In this chapter, we will find that this worldview unites Christology, ecclesiology, and soteriology in a way that Christ's mission becomes His people's through His Emmanuel presence with them until His final return.

### The Resurrection as the Basis for Faith

It is no coincidence that the chapter that gives us the Great Commission begins with the empty tomb. "In the end of the sabbath, as it began to dawn toward the first day of the week, came Mary Magdalene and the other Mary to see the sepulchre. And, behold, there was a great earthquake: for the angel of the Lord descended from heaven, and came and rolled back the stone from the door, and sat upon it. His countenance was like lightning, and his raiment white as snow: and for fear of him the keepers did shake, and became as dead men" (Matt. 28:1–4).

The resurrection of Jesus Christ came on the heels of the crucifixion of Christ, and shows not only the truth of Christ's own words (Matt. 16:21), but also the glorious answer of heaven to the work of Christ. In other words, now it is clear to all the world that "he shall save his people from their sins" (Matt. 1:21). And so the resurrection sends news everywhere. The angels tell the women. The women tell the disciples, and Christ himself comes to send the news outward. And the news goes everywhere. In other words, the resurrection

sends this gospel outward, because life has conquered death. There is good news to tell other sinners around us.

There is no Christian worldview without the truth of the resurrection. Much of our Western world celebrates Easter, but does the truth that Jesus Christ rose from the dead shape how we look at the world? Now the tomb doesn't negate the reality of death, as some people like to think it does. It isn't just some sort of optimistic miracle that shows us that everything turns out okay in the end. The believer reckons with the truth that Christ died, having been crucified for the offenses of His people, but also that He was raised in order that His salvation might be applied by Him through His Spirit. The tidings of His death and resurrection should go throughout the world, where sin and death have had their grip on all. This gospel speaks and lives the news of this conquering Savior.

Because this tomb outside of Jerusalem is empty, Christians can live in newness of life. While it is true that without Him we can do nothing, it is equally true that engrafted into Him, and by His strength we can do all things. Are you a partaker of Christ and all His benefits by a living faith? Without Him, death stares us in the face. But engrafted into Him, His resurrection power works in ar through us and we can do His will and bring glory to His name Rom. 6:4). We can go forward not with carnal weapons, but i strength of promised grace and with the full assurance that J is in us is greater than he that is in the world, to pull dow holds, cast down imaginations, and every high thing that e against the knowledge of God (2 Cor. 10:4–5).

### The Lies of Those Who Deny the Faith

Matthew 28, the chapter in which we find the Gr
also mentions lies. In verses 11–15, we read of the
been guarding the tomb, being bribed by the Je
ers: "Now when they were going, behold, so·
into the city, and shewed unto the chief pr
were done. And when they were assemble·
taken counsel, they gave large money ur
ye, His disciples came by night, and st·
And if this come to the governor's e·
secure you. So they took the money, a.

this saying is commonly reported among the Jews until this day". In other words, these guards were paid to tell a lie about the resurrection, to deny it. They were to say that Jesus's body had been stolen from the tomb by His disciples while the guards slept. This lie gained a lot of ground, so much so that it was reported at the time of the writing of Matthew's gospel (Matt. 28:15).

It's no coincidence that the Great Commission comes on the heels, as it were, of this denial of the truth of the resurrection, and therefore, a denial of the truth of the gospel itself. This lie was its own "alternate commission" of sorts. It was conjured up to sound plausible. It said to people: "The church, and its leaders, are promoting a hoax. What they are telling you is nonsense. Just go back to your sinful lives, to the mirage of hopes or the pessimism of despair. Don't bother with Christians. They have made it all up. We have people who will vouch for the real facts."

These lies are still being promulgated, and there is still lots of money behind them. There is university money, media money, science money, political money. There are many voices trying to portray the church, and Christianity, as a hoax, or something that people latch onto when they don't have anything else. Christians are portrayed as non-intellectuals, as people who believe fantasies and wishful thinking.

Until we recognize that lies are being promoted all around us, we won't realize the offensiveness and relevance of the Great Commission. We need to recognize that there is a great and massively funded effort aimed squarely at taking on the Christian gospel. While believers are seeking to live and work in conformity with the great Commission, others are just as energetically working against gospel. Christianity is not just another voice of so-called truth, of a buffet that people can pick from as they please. There is only truth that stands this lie on its head, and unmasks it for what it is. here are seasons in most of our lives when we grow discour- when we recognize a well-funded, prominent, and powerful ent combatting the truth. We can be depressed and paralyzed But rather than be paralyzed, let's be energized by the fact e are both lies that need to be exposed, and this truth that be proclaimed.

What lies are swirling around us today? What lies do we need to expose? There's the lie of evolution, that the world originated somewhere other than in God's creating decree. There's the lie of syncretism—telling us that all religions lead to God. "Feel free to mix them as you see fit," we're told. There's the pro-choice lie, which tells us that every child deserves to be "planned and wanted." There is the lie of relativism, which tells us that there is no absolute truth, right or wrong. There are countless other lies—lies like individualism, socialism, consumerism, ritualism, materialism. We could say it like this, "Hell has its commission: go and make prisoners through these lies. Heaven says: go and make disciples with the truth."

## The Doubt of Those Who Need More Faith

There is a nugget in verse 17 that needs some attention. We read in verses 16 and 17: "Then the eleven disciples went away into Galilee, into a mountain where Jesus had appointed them. And when they saw him, they worshipped him: but some doubted." In other words, some of the disciples who saw Jesus after His resurrection doubted that it was indeed Him! Thankfully, not all of them did, but we are told that "some doubted"! Isn't this amazing that, while the authorities were boldly making up lies about Jesus's resurrection, there was timidity and doubt among the disciples?

I have often wondered why God has seen fit to include this mention of doubters in Scripture. One reason, I believe, is it gives us a realistic picture of believers, of followers of Christ. Isn't the Bible remarkably honest about people? It tells us about Simon Peter's denial, about the discouragement of the men on the road to Emmaus (Luke 24:13–24), about the doubt of Thomas (John 20:20–29), one of the twelve, after the resurrection. And here we're told that "some doubted." We are certainly given a realistic picture of the people who are the church of God. God is honest about us in order that our confidence would not be in ourselves, but in God who raises the dead to life. There are many today, also in the church, who doubt.

Perhaps as you read this, you are one of these people who is so easily tossed back and forth. You wish it were different. When you are honest, you confess that you doubt. Allow me to say this: the Great Commission isn't just for those who have a super-faith, for the strongest of believers. God also gives it to those who often struggle with doubts and fears. Like Timothy, we may be of a timid spirit and a feeble mind. But God uses weak things to confound the wise (1 Cor. 1:27). When a timid disciple steps out in faith to speak about Christ to neighbors, loved ones, children, parents, or friends, it isn't the steadfastness of the faith of the person that makes the ultimate difference, but the steadfastness of the truth that the person witnesses to.

It's true: God has to remind us that we have not been given "the spirit of fear; but of power, and of love, and of a sound mind" (2 Tim. 1:7). His grace is sufficient for us and it is in the midst of our weakness that His strength is made known. Christ thus says to all His doubting and fearful disciples, "Be not afraid" (John 6:20) but rather "be of good cheer; I have overcome the world" (John 16:33). We can trust Him, for He has promised that He will never leave us nor forsake us. He is with us always, even unto the end of the world. He sends out His people to make disciples in spite of their own doubts and fears and promises them His presence with them to carry them through whatever difficulties they are likely to meet with. He orders it so that the excellence of the power may be of God and not of man (2 Cor. 4:7).

The story is told of John Livingston, a Covenanter in Scotland in the year 1630 at the young age of 27. During a communion season, he was asked to preach on a Monday, in a post-communion service. Here, he says, "there came such a misgiving of spirit upon me, considering my unworthiness and weakness, and the multitude and expectation of the people, that I was consulting with myself to have stolen away somewhere."[1] He did in fact try to run from the scene, away from the task he'd been asked to do, because of his fear. But the Lord impressed on his mind the following words from Jeremiah: "Have I been a wilderness unto Israel? a land of darkness?" (Jer. 2:31) Thereupon Livingston went back and preached with such divine blessing that five hundred credible conversions took place on that occasion. What an example of how God is able to use a doubting believer, that all the glory might be His!

None of this is to encourage or excuse our doubts; rather, to encourage us to look to the Lord who can turn doubters into those who confess His name! From a doubting Thomas, the Lord can bring

---

1. John Livingston, *A Brief Historical Relation, of the Life of Mr. John Livingston... Written by Himself, Etc.* (Reprint; Edinburgh: John Johnstone, 1848), 19–21.

forth the magnificent disciple-making confession: "My LORD and my God" (John 20:28). Such is the strength and power of Christ.

## The Supremacy of Christ as the Object of Faith

It is Christ who is ultimately center-stage in the worldview that conforms to the Great Commission. It is, after all, His commission. He decrees as King of kings and Lord of lords. All things are under Him, as He makes abundantly clear: "All power is given unto me in heaven and in earth" (Matt. 28:18). There are at least four things in this statement about Christ's supremacy:

1. It is a *complete* supremacy. He leaves nothing out of the "all." He doesn't share this supremacy with another. God has indeed highly exalted Him and given Him to be a Prince and a Savior. All power is His!

2. It is a *comprehensive* supremacy. It covers both "heaven and earth." We need not wonder what the forces beyond us might do. They are all under the control of Christ who rules from heaven and rules both heaven and earth. Moreover, He rules the whole of the earth, no part excepted.

3. It is *Christ's* supremacy. It has been given to Him by the Father based on His finished work. It is no stranger on the throne of heaven. It is the same Savior who walked the earth and taught His disciples, did miracles and signs, who is now on the throne of heaven. The Father has given it to Him and will never remove it from Him.

4. It is a *commissioning* supremacy. How does Christ use this supremacy? Many things could be mentioned, for Christ is over all, as Revelation makes clear: all developments in history and all judgment to come at the end of time. But Matthew focuses us first of all on the gospel cause. Christ uses His supremacy evangelistically. "Go ye therefore, and teach all nations" (Matt. 28:19).

The Great Commission is not something the apostles thought up as some sort of strategy for post-resurrection mission work. Instead, this commission has the full weight of Christ's authority in heaven and earth behind it. And only the authority of almighty God enables us to obey it. The call must go forth that people from all nations forsake all other refuges and put their hope for salvation in God alone.

As John Calvin says, by nothing other than divine authority could Jesus "command us to promise eternal life in his name, to reduce the whole world under his sway, and to publish a doctrine which subdues all pride, and lays prostrate the whole of the human race."[2]

As you seek to obey the Great Commission, does your worldview include an understanding of the absolute authority of Christ? He is the sovereign Lord of the universe, having absolute and universal power. All things happen according to the dictates of His will. Everything that comes to pass has been foreordained and happens in His way and in His time. He does according to the counsel of His will in the army of heaven and among the inhabitants of the earth. He has been given *all* power in heaven and earth to do so, and we can rest assured therefore that He will build His church in spite of every effort of men or devils to hinder and frustrate the mission of God.

The early church operated on the basis of Christ's sovereign authority as we see in Acts 1:8. So, too, the church today must minister in His name and look to Him in dependence upon His power and guidance. We do not face a lost world on the basis of our own authority, but on the basis of the absolute authority of our King and Head, Jesus Christ.

Believers, this authority should both empower us and energize us. We might think of how divine sovereignty and human responsibility are both evident in missions, just as a farmer plows his field, sows the seed, and fertilizes the ground—all the while knowing that, in the end, he cannot cause the seed to grow, he cannot produce the rain and sunshine the plants need, and he cannot bring about a successful harvest. He is dependent on God for these things. But the famer also knows that, unless he works diligently, plowing, planting, fertilizing, and cultivating, he cannot expect a harvest at the end of the season. The farmer will reap the benefits of this venture only if he has fulfilled his responsibilities. The farmer cannot do what God must do, and God will not do what the farmer should do.

So, too, in the gospel cause we may not shirk our responsibilities. God has ordained that men and women from all nations are to be saved, but he has also ordained the means to that end. The gospel is

---

2. John Calvin, *A Commentary on the Harmony of the Evangelists, Matthew, Mark, and Luke*, Vol. 3; trans. William Pringle (Edinburgh: Calvin Translation Society, 1846), 381.

therefore to be preached in all nations as the power of God unto salvation. Let us therefore work together with God for the furtherance of the gospel in our own day and generation believing that God is not slack concerning His promises but that He is the same God still, true to His word, and He will bring to pass all that He has purposed through His own divinely appointed means.

## Following Christ by Faith

The Great Commission focuses preeminently on disciple-making, that is to say, making followers of Christ (Matt. 28:19). Let's think for a few moments about what following Christ means. It means that we are to walk as Christ walked, adorning the doctrine of God our Savior with a servant-like, God-glorifying life. We are called to present a winsome and authentic Christianity that puts Christ on display to those around us. This means we are by grace to seek to cultivate a Christ-likeness. We are not to love in word only, but in deed and in truth. We are to walk uprightly, with integrity and consistency, in wisdom toward them that are without, with an earnest desire to see all men brought into the kingdom of God's dear Son. Our lives ought to be a living epistle to the reality of grace, clearly showing that it alone has the power to transform lives and satisfy the longings of the human heart. It ought to be clear that our citizenship is in heaven and that we are not wed to this world or the things that are in it. In all these ways, we are to live lives that become the gospel and hold forth the word of life that others might be drawn to Christ. Only as we follow Christ wholly and live authentic Christian lives that speak of His love and grace can we expect that others will be drawn to Christ. No matter where we are, we should be witnesses for Jesus Christ and seek to draw and win others to Him (Acts 11:19–21).

Let's remind ourselves also of this important truth as we seek to follow Christ: following Christ will be a humbling and self-sacrificing life. Are we taking up our cross, and denying ourselves, that we might follow after Him? Is this kind of following part of our worldview? We are to adopt the mentality and outlook of a servant, not living unto ourselves but unto Him who loved us and gave Himself for us. We are not to seek our own but the things that are Christ's, seeking first His kingdom and His righteousness.

We follow Christ, for His mission is our mission. "As my Father hath sent me, even so send I you" (John 20:21). What a glorious send-off that would have been from the Father to the Son! And Christ gives us to follow in His footsteps. This is the highest honor!

To put it simply—what is the worldview of a follower? It is seeing everything through the lens of Christ Himself. He goes before; He leads the way. He shows us where the safe path is. He identifies the obstacles and leads His people over them and through them. To conform our worldview to the Great Commission is to follow Christ personally, unconditionally, and practically.

### The Presence of Christ through Faith

Finally, Christ includes a profound encouragement in this Great Commission: "Lo, I am with you always" (Matt. 28:20).

Can we imagine a more comforting truth than to have the Savior with us? As the disciples of Christ engage in the direction of their Lord and Master, they have the assurance that He will come along. In fact, He will never leave them. He will be among them, in their midst, no matter what happens.

Have you ever noticed that thus the gospel of Matthew comes full circle? Back in Chapter 1 of his book, Matthew records the angel's appearance to Joseph, telling him that not only will the child's name be Jesus, "for he shall save his people from their sins" (Matt. 1:21). "They shall call his name Emmanuel, which being interpreted is, God with us" (Matt. 1:23). In other words, people will realize by faith over and over again that Jesus is "God with us." As they submit to His Word, His yoke, and His truth, they will acknowledge this glorious doctrine and celebrate it. They will pass it on to others so that they too will know Him and God's presence through Him.

What is more, when Christ leaves His church physically, He is never absent from them. In fact, He is with them always, or as the original language indicates, every day until the very end. That is a glorious comfort. That means that there is not a time when Christ is not present with His church. He is there when missions are going well. He is there when persecution is horrible. He is there when their faith is strong. He is there when their faith grows weak. He is with them on the sunny days as well as the cloudy ones, the glad days as well as the sad, the prosperous days as well as the difficult.

The worldview of the Great Commission is not a worldview that sees the Christian alone on some sort of lonely mission frontier. No, far from it! God is with us in Christ. That defines our world. And this Christ meets us through His Word and Spirit, like He did those women on the way: "Jesus met them, saying, All hail" (Matt. 28:9). He meets us as we gather together in the appointed places of worship, and He draws close to us, and shows us He is with us. He is our worldview as He enables us to view our world. He Himself is the window to our world.

# CHAPTER 9

# Looking unto Jesus in This World to Follow Him into the Next
### Hebrews 12:1-3

*Charles M. Barrett*

Faith in Jesus Christ, the Son of God, occupies an essential role in a Christian worldview. Much of what forms the basis and framework of a Christian worldview remains unseen by the physical eye. Faith, however, is the substance of things hoped for, the evidence of things not seen (Heb. 11:1). Faith is no mere make-believe. It rests upon the objective truth of God's Word. The Heidelberg Catechism teaches us that true faith "is not only a certain knowledge, whereby I hold for truth all that God has revealed to us in His Word, but also an assured confidence, which the Holy Ghost works by the gospel in my heart…" (Q. 21). Three important elements of faith are highlighted in this definition: (1) faith rests upon God's Word, (2) faith involves knowledge and trust, and (3) the Holy Ghost works faith in us. While unseen realities shape our worldview, they are certain and true because God reveals them to us in His Word and works in us by His Holy Spirit knowledge and trust. The Book of Hebrews reveals to us vital truths that we embrace by faith in order to live by faith as we navigate the circumstances of this life.

The emphasis that Hebrews places upon living by faith makes this book vital for formulating a worldview. The book is important not only as part of the authoritative canon, but also because of its genre within the canon. Hebrews is a sermon.[1] The writer reminds his audience in his conclusion that this is a "word of exhortation" (Heb. 13:22).[2] As a sermon Hebrews reminds believers that the worship of

---

1. Anthony T. Selvaggio, "Preaching Advice from the 'Sermon' to the Hebrews," *Themelios* 32, no. 2 (2006): 33.

2. The same phrase in the Greek is used by Paul in Acts 13:15 to describe his preaching.

God and the active sitting under the preached Word is necessary to our Christian walk and worldview. Hebrews is a divinely inspired sermon preached to believers who found themselves persecuted for their faith in Christ and tempted to fall back and return to their former way of life. The central message of the sermon is to persevere in your walk by looking unto Jesus, who is the author and finisher of your faith. This essay will consider how Hebrews 12:1–3 encourages us to follow Jesus into the next life by looking unto him in this life. After considering the call to look to Jesus in Hebrews 12, we will review how Hebrews as a whole encourages us to see Jesus by faith.

## The Call to Follow (Hebrews 12:1–3)

*A Lesson in History*

Hebrews exhorts Christians to run a race involving hardships and difficulties. The present trials, however, ought not to be the focal point of the believer. Rather, we run with patience the course that God sets for us, looking unto Jesus (12:1–2). Such running involves faith and trust in the God who does all things right. The exhortation to run immediately follows a sustained history lesson in God's faithfulness to His people in the Old Testament (Hebrews 11). In a remarkably succinct summary of redemptive history, Hebrews traces God's divine intervention and protection of His children who ran their race by looking forward to their eternal hope. While many of the examples given ended well with regard to the stated trial, many did not, at least from a human perspective. It is exciting to recall how God preserved Noah, guided Abraham in his sojourn, provided a child to Sarah, delivered Isaac, blessed Jacob, raised Joseph to prominence, worked marvelous deeds through Moses, knocked down the walls of Jericho, and redeemed the harlot Rahab. Those stories inspire the Christian to persevere through hardships. Hebrews 11 continues with amazing exploits of judges, kings, and prophets who subdued kingdoms, wrought righteousness, obtained promises, stopped the mouths of lions, quenched the violence of fire, escaped the edge of the sword, out of weakness were made strong, waxed valiant in battle, and more (11:32–35).

But not every act of faith in the sovereign God ended well in the moment, at least as far as a naturalistic or materialistic worldview is concerned. Some were stoned, some were sawn in half, were tempted, were slain with the sword (11:37). Yet, they received their reward along with those whose stories ended well in the moment. This juxtaposition of immediate deliverance and martyrdom teaches us something important about faith and about how we are to run the race set before us. The efficacy of faith is not in how a particular trial ends since faith's ultimate goal rests upon something beyond the trial. Faith rests in God who promises something better for us than mere escape. He promises for us eternal citizenship in a better city where we dwell with Him forever. The past's faithful encompass us as a cloud of witnesses reminding us that God always brings His children home. He is faithful and wise in the course He sets for each of His children. The past encourages us in the present and motivates us to run with patience.

*The Manner of Running*

Faith does not trust in some abstract idea of God. Faith rests upon Jesus, who is the author and finisher of our faith. A Christian, by God's grace, fixes his eyes upon Jesus Christ during the run. When Christ is the object He will undoubtedly govern and dictate how we run. As the pioneer and end of our faith we are encouraged that He is also the upholder of our faith. Our faith finds its source, its middle, and its end in Jesus Christ. This influences our run. When the object of our faith induces within us greater delight than what is around us, we have the motivation to run with an eternal perspective with a focus that is before us and above us. Hebrews reminds us that looking to Jesus propels us to a willingness to lay things aside for the sake of our run. We run by laying aside weights and sins.

The writer employs vivid imagery in his athletic metaphor. The one running must lay aside anything that would impede or encumber the run. It is disastrous to retain something that might hinder us from reaching our goal.[3] The weight we lay aside may not be wrong in and of itself. Though permissible, it may impede our running. We are to be more desirous of reaching our goal than we are to retain what has the potential to encumber.

---

3. Paul Ellingworth, *The Epistle to the Hebrews: A Commentary on the Greek Text*, New International Greek Testament Commentary (Grand Rapids; Carlisle: Eerdmans; Paternoster Press, 1993), 639.

I do not know much about running. Though certainly not an expert, I know a little more about cycling. There are similarities between the metaphor Hebrews employs and cycling. Where I live there are a lot of hills. Climbing these hills is not easy. Every ounce shed makes for a slightly easier climb, so I am always looking for ways to lay aside any weight I can. Unfortunately, there are few easy shortcuts to lighten the load. I informed my wife one day about the wonders of newer carbon bikes with lighter components than I currently had and how a newer bike would improve my already limited climbing ability. She perceptively asked about both the cost of an upgrade and precisely how much lighter a new bike would be than the almost new bike I have. With great excitement, trying to sell the idea, I said the upgrade would be about one pound lighter (maybe even one and a half) at a cost of approximately $1,500. She kindly reminded me that I could lose fifteen pounds by laying aside donuts and possibly that second piece of pie. She was right. I had to determine whether climbing a hill with greater ease was more important to me than donuts. It was, and the better health and looser pants are not too bad either. The point is, we must be willing to lay aside anything that might hinder the goal before us.

John Owen suggests four practical insights regarding the laying aside of good things.[4] First, it is not required that we should part with them permanently, or absolutely. There may be seasons in life that we need to lay even good things aside for the sake of the run. Second, the believer must be willing to lay aside things. A lack of willingness exposes the threat that could come upon the runner by holding on to things too dearly. Third, laying aside encumbrances requires diligent attentiveness to what needs to be mortified. Running well warrants careful preparation and focus, knowing what will help and what will hinder. Fourth, laying aside hindrances requires continual observation. We run conscientiously daily. There are no shortcuts in the Christian life. Believers must be diligent and vigilant.

Not only are Christians to lay aside the weights that encumber and slow us, we are also exhorted to lay aside the sin that so easily besets. Sin is twisted and destructive. Letting sin run rampant in our

---

4. John Owen, *An Exposition of the Epistle to the Hebrews*, ed. W. H. Goold, vol. 24, Works of John Owen (Edinburgh: Johnstone and Hunter, 1854), 226–27.

lives will threaten us and cause disastrous consequences.[5] Throughout the Old and New Testaments God warns us of the dangers of sin. Paul instructs Christians to put off the old man and put on the new (Ephesians 4 and Colossians 3). Peter does the same (1 Peter 2:1), as well as reminds us of the adversary who seeks to devour (1 Peter 5:8). We run wisely by confessing our sin, fighting our sin, and never trifling with sin. Sin trips the runner. With fierce dedication we run patiently, looking unto Jesus.

*Looking unto Jesus*

Jesus is our Savior and our example (Heb. 12:2). The order is of great importance.[6] Before encouraging believers to consider Jesus and His faithful and obedient life, Hebrews reminds us that Jesus is the author and finisher of our faith. He is the object of our trust and the hope of our salvation. Being redeemed, we can consider the course that was set before Him in order to find encouragement and motivation in our race. Just as Christ endured the cross for the joy that was set before Him, so we can persevere in our providentially set course by remembering the joy that will be ours at the finish line. Jesus endured the cross and its shame for the joy of exaltation that awaited Him. We, like Jesus and because of Jesus, will also experience the joy of exaltation and full redemption. Like an Olympic sprinter who fixes her eyes on the finish line, so we fix the eye of faith upon Jesus. We are called to live a life of faith by consistently looking unto Jesus. We read this exhortation and encouragement in chapter 12, but the entire book instructs us how to look to Jesus.

## How to Look to Jesus in This Life

The call to live by faith, to look unto, and to consider Jesus permeates the book from the very beginning. Hebrews exhorts us to fix our faith upon the all-sufficient Savior and to reject any temptation to turn away from Him. Hebrews sets Christ before the readers in an unmistakable way so that by chapter 12 we know where to look

5. Richard D. Phillips, *Hebrews*, ed. Richard D. Phillips, Philip Graham Ryken, and Daniel M. Doriani, Reformed Expository Commentary (Phillipsburg, N.J.: P&R Publishing, 2006), 532.

6. See J. Gresham Machen, *The Origin of Paul's Religion* (New York: The Macmillan Company, 1921) for a defense of orthodoxy over liberalism, which attempts to place a primary role on Jesus as an example.

and what to consider. What follows is a broad view of the way this inspired sermon presents the blessedness of Christ.

### Consider the Glory of His Person

Hebrews opens with a glorious description of the beauty and excellence of Christ's Person. In the first six verses God confronts us with four features of His Son that captivate our attention and elicit the proper response of trust. The original audience faced severe trials and testing. Many felt the pull to turn their backs on the Christian faith. Like them, Christians of every generation encounter the temptation to return to their former way of life. Pressures can bear down and raise the possibility that life might just be better if they did not follow Christ. Hebrews counters this temptation and the fallacy that turning away brings blessedness. Christ is supreme over all things and indescribably beautiful in His Person.

The first feature for our consideration is that Jesus Christ is God's final revelation (Heb. 1:1–2). God spoke in former days to His people by the prophets. He spoke in the last days by His Son. It is remarkable that God speaks to us at all. In fact, at the foundation of a Christian worldview is the belief that God is and God has spoken. God has not left us to ourselves without a word. So many today venture on a quest for truth and knowledge, yet ignore and reject the source of all truth. He speaks truth and sets us free. What is more, given who He is and who we are it is a wonder that He speaks to us words of love, grace, and mercy. When Adam and Eve fell into sin we could expect a word of immediate wrath and swift condemnation. Yet, we hear God calling out for Adam and Eve and within the word of cursing there is a word of promise and salvation (Gen. 3:15). The progressive revelation of this promise comes from God through the prophets to the people.

All that God spoke to the fathers by the prophets was true. But it was not final. His words in the former days were promissory. The prophets were mere men and contained no authority in their own right. And no one prophet was able to provide a word that expressed the fullness of God's revelation. The revelation of the former days carried within it a progressive element and an inherent anticipation. Promise turned to fulfillment, and the partial turned to full when God sent forth His Son, made of a woman, made under the law (Gal. 4:4).

When Jesus came to earth He fulfilled what was formerly spoken. He did not bring a message different from the Old Testament and inaugurate a new religion. God spoke to the fathers through the prophets a word that concerned Jesus Christ. Hebrews affirms this by its frequent citations and allusions to the Old Testament Scriptures. There is continuity between the Old and the New. Jesus is the final and full revelation of God because He comes from the Father (John 5:36) and speaks the words His Father commanded Him to speak (John 12:49). In Jesus we receive all that we need to know, and in Him are hid all the treasures of wisdom and knowledge (Col. 2:3). Considering Jesus as the final revelation of God the Father we have all that we need to persevere in the faith, not turning aside to anything else. To turn from Jesus is to turn from the truth and to turn from God's revelation. Such a turning would be disastrous and folly. As we run the course God the Father sovereignly sets before us, let us do so looking unto Jesus who is God's final revelation. In Him we have all we need.

Second, we ought to consider Jesus the Lord of the universe. Hebrews 1:2–3 point to the Son who is the agent of creation ("by whom also he made the worlds"), the goal of creation ("whom he hath appointed heir of all things"), and the sustainer of creation ("upholding all things by the word of his power"). Throughout the struggles and trials of this life we are to look to the One who is Lord of all. There is nothing outside of Christ's possession, nothing exists that was not made by Him, and nothing is upheld that is not sustained by His power. This feature strengthens our faith in the midst of chaos, confusion, and persecution. What may be chaotic and confusing to us is not outside the control of Christ. He does not get confused, nor does He experience angst or dread. Jesus is the One to whom we can look in our race and unreservedly trust.

The third feature our attention is drawn to is that Jesus is "the brightness of [the Father's] glory, and the express image of his person" (1:3). Jesus enjoys all the blessedness of perfections that belong to God. We know that God is infinite, eternal, and unchangeable in His being, wisdom, power, holiness, justice, goodness, and truth.[7] Jesus reveals these attributes as the brightness of God's glory and

---

7. *Westminster Shorter Catechism*, Question 4.

person. We see this remarkable truth when we consider Jesus's inter-action with His disciples in the Upper Room (John 14). He comforted His disciples in the midst of confusion and encouraged them not to let their hearts be troubled. They believed in God; they were to believe also in Jesus. He told them that He is the way, the life, and the truth. The way to the Father is through Jesus. Philip responded with his stated desire to see the Father. Such a sight would certainly satisfy the troubled believer. Jesus's reply summarizes the truth of Hebrews 1:3. Jesus said, "Have I been so long time with you, and yet hast thou not known me, Philip? He that hath seen me hath seen the Father" (John 14:9). Jesus is the radiance of the Father. When we run looking unto Jesus we see by faith the glory and brightness of the blessedness of God.

The fourth and final feature that confronts us is Jesus as the proper object of worship (Heb. 1:4–6). To worship anything other than God is idolatry. The writer observes that Jesus is so much better than the angels as He has obtained a more excellent name than they (1:4). God never said to the angels, "Thou art my Son." Yet, He has said that to Jesus. What is more, the angels of God worship Him (1:6). God alone is worthy of worship. And Jesus, who is God's final revelation, the Lord of all things, and the brightness of the Father's glory, is the object of our worship. These realities correspond to the way in which we are to live the Christian life. Jesus is God's final revelation, so hear Him. Jesus is the Lord of the universe, so trust Him. Jesus is the brightness of the Father's glory, so know and delight in Him. Jesus is the object of worship, so praise Him. Each reality encourages us to endure in this life by looking unto Jesus, who is glorious in His Person.

### Consider the Wonder of Christ's Work

The exhortation to look unto Jesus draws our focus upon the work of our Savior. The author intentionally uses the name *Jesus*. His name is Jesus because He will save His people from their sins. As we run the Christian race by faith we are to look to the One who loved us and gave Himself for us. We are to look to the wonder of Christ's work in His incarnation, His sacrifice, and His intercession. These are certainly not the only aspects of Christ's work Hebrews addresses.[8]

---

8. For example, Hebrews also discusses Christ's obedience in His life, the resur-rection, and the ascension. There is also extensive treatment on His priestly ministry

Given the nature of this message, we can only be suggestive with the works mentioned. May these realities of Christ's ministry motivate you to further study, contemplation, and meditation upon Christ's saving work for you.

*The Son Who Took on Flesh*
The wonder of Christ's Person expounded and presented in Hebrews 1 prepares us to behold the wonder of Christ's work detailed in chapter 2. God did not put the world in subjection to the angels (2:5). Rather, God put the world to come in subjection to a man. Citing Psalm 8, the writer identifies Jesus as the man He was mindful of, the Son of Man that He visited (2:6). The eternal Son of God, the brightness of the Father's glory, was made a little lower than the angels (2:7, 9). What marvelous wonder and grace! It became the Son, for whom and by whom are all things (2:10) to partake of flesh and blood (2:14). Several Old Testament passages are quoted in order to show that Jesus Christ took on flesh in order to express solidarity with humanity. He is not ashamed to call us brethren (Matt. 28:10; Heb. 2:11). The Son of God did not take on only part of man's nature, but the entirety of it.

The Westminster Confession of Faith (8.2) confesses the Son of God took upon Himself man's nature, "with all the essential properties, and common infirmities thereof, yet without sin." He endured in the flesh all kinds of temptations and sufferings, being touched with the feeling of our infirmities (Heb. 2:18; 4:15). As our Mediator, it was necessary that He take on flesh. Hebrews even asks, "Who can have compassion on the ignorant, and on them that are out of the way; for that he himself also is compassed with infirmity" (5:2). It behooved Him to be made like His brethren (2:17). Jesus lived His earthly life by faith in God and obedience to His Father (Heb. 10:7–10). So we are to live by faith and walk in obedience. We do so looking unto Jesus who is the author and the finisher of our faith. Jesus blazed the trail before us in His flesh.

*The Son Who Made Himself a Sacrifice*
There is almost an ascending scale of wonder as we look to Jesus. We see Him first in the flesh and stand in awe of the great condescension

---

that extends beyond our consideration of the main acts of sacrifice and intercession (Heb. 4–10).

of the eternal Son of God who took on our nature. But such wonder only intensifies as we consider the reason for which He came. He came to die. He was made a little lower than the angels *for* the suffering of death and that He should taste death for every man (2:9). It was necessary that He might be made the captain of our salvation through suffering (2:10). He took part of the same flesh and blood of humanity that He might destroy the devil *through* death. Jesus took on human nature that He might redeem humanity through death.

If the Son did not take on human nature, then there would be no salvation. If the Son did not suffer and die, then there would be no salvation for mankind. He did not take on the nature of angels. He took on the nature of the seed of Abraham that He might take them to glory (2:16). Hebrews develops the sacrificial nature of Jesus's ministry from the perspective of the priestly office (chapters 4–10). Jesus's priesthood is compared and contrasted with that of the Levitical priesthood (chapter 7). The priesthood of the older covenant was inherently weak (7:11–19). The priest himself needed first to make a sacrifice for himself and then for others (7:27). Jesus, on the other hand, is holy, harmless, undefiled, separate from sinners, and made higher than the heavens (7:26). He did not need to first offer sacrifices for Himself (7:27). He had no sin in Himself for which to atone. But that is not the only difference. It is not as though, because of His perfection, He got to skip that first step and move immediately to offering a lamb or goat for us. No! He offered Himself as the sacrifice (7:27). This is the great wonder of redemption. The eternal Son of God took on flesh in order to lay down His own life as a sacrifice for the sins of His people. By shedding His blood Jesus offers a perfect sacrifice that brings perfect and complete redemption for His people (Heb. 9–10).

We run with clean consciences before God as we consider the Christ who died for us. Because Christ came in the flesh, lived a holy life in the flesh, died an atoning death in the flesh, and rose again the third day in the flesh, we have full redemption and remission of sins (9:22). What greater motivation to run and lay aside weights and sin than the death of Jesus for us? What greater motivation than to see the love of God manifest toward us in that He sent His Son to die? Hugh Martin expressed the glory of the connection between God's love, the incarnation, and the sacrifice well. He said, "It is the shedding of Christ's blood which proves the love of God. For without shedding of blood there is no such transaction of marvelous, infinite, peculiar, and sovereign love as the true and valid remission of sin—remission in the gift and death of 'God manifest in the flesh'—implies."[9] Dear Christian, consider the Son who made Himself a sacrifice for you as you live by faith.

*The Son Who Intercedes for You*
The Christian life is often hard. Hebrews is written to encourage us to continue and persevere despite the challenges and oppositions we face. There is no comfort in turning back because there is nothing like living and dying for Jesus. Yet, as we run we are not only called to consider the work of Christ in the past or the prospect of eternity with Christ in the future. We are also called to consider the intercessory ministry of Christ in the present. In some sense, there is no facet of time—past, present, or future—where we cannot consider Jesus. He who lived, died, rose again, ascended, and sat down is active on our behalf even now. Jesus has passed through the heavens and in His flesh has sat down at the right hand of the Father (1:3; 4:14). And Hebrews tells us what Jesus is doing. Because of His unchangeable priesthood, "he is able...to save them to the uttermost...seeing he ever liveth to make intercession for [His people] (7:25)."

Christians endure to the end, in part, because Jesus prays for them. The wonder of Christ's intercession for His people is that it continues even when we are not conscious of it. We often ask our friends at church to pray for us. And we hope they remember. Christ, however, lives to intercede for His people. When we sleep, when we are awake, when we are in the deep waters of affliction, Jesus prays for His people. Just as He did with Peter, Jesus prays that our faith would not fail. When the trials of life test us and we cannot see a way past those trials, Jesus prays for us. As you run with patience, look unto Jesus who prays for you. As you encounter dangers that lurk about you, remember that Jesus is praying for you.

**Conclusion**
Hebrews identifies various dangers that can hinder our race. There is the failure to heed what Christ has done (2:1). There is the failure to

---

9. Hugh Martin, *The Atonement: In Its Relations to the Covenant, the Priesthood, the Intercession of Our Lord* (Edinburgh: James Gemmell, 1882), 191.

go forward to maturity and to fall away (6:1–8). And there is failure to finish the race (12). So run, heeding what Christ has done, going forward to maturity, and finishing the race set before you. To the one who looks to Jesus, we say with the preacher of Hebrews, "Beloved, we are persuaded better things of you, and things that accompany salvation" (6:9). There is a sovereignly appointed course set for you by a loving Father. He has given His Son Jesus to be all that you need in this race. Live by faith in the One who began it and will finish it. May your worldview be shaped more by what you see by faith than what you see by sight. Look ever unto Jesus in this life that you may enjoy eternal bliss with Him in the next.

# Contributors

**CHARLES BARRETT** is assistant minister at Wayside Presbyterian Church (PCA) in Signal Mountain, Tennessee. He also serves as Adjunct Professor at Belhaven University, Chattanooga.

**MICHAEL BARRETT** is Vice President for Academic Affairs/Academic Dean, and Professor of Old Testament at Puritan Reformed Theological Seminary. He serves as an ordained minister of the Heritage Reformed Congregations.

**JOEL R. BEEKE** is President and Professor of Systematic Theology and Homiletics at Puritan Reformed Theological Seminary. He also serves as a pastor of the Heritage Reformed Congregation in Grand Rapids, Michigan.

**GERALD BILKES** is Professor of New Testament and Biblical Theology at Puritan Reformed Theological Seminary. An ordained minister in the Free Reformed churches, he also preaches regularly in the USA and Canada.

**BRIAN COSBY** serves as senior pastor of Wayside Presbyterian Church (PCA) on Signal Mountain, Tennessee. He is also Visiting Professor at Reformed Theological Seminary, Atlanta, and Adjunct Professor at Belhaven University, Chattanooga.

**MARK KELDERMAN** serves as Dean of Students and Spiritual Formation, as well as Instructor in Pastoral Theology, at Puritan Reformed Theological Seminary. He serves as an ordained minister of the Heritage Reformed Congregations.

**PAUL M. SMALLEY** is Faculty Teaching Assistant to Joel Beeke at Puritan Reformed Theological Seminary. He also serves as a bi-vocational pastor at Grace Immanuel Reformed Baptist Church in Grand Rapids, Michigan.

**DEREK W. H. THOMAS** is the senior minister at First Presbyterian Church (ARP) in Columbia, South Carolina. He is also the Robert Strong Professor of Systematic and Pastoral Theology at Reformed Theological Seminary, Atlanta.